The Stage Is All the World

THE THEATRICAL DESIGNS OF TANYA MOISEIWITSCH

The Stage Is All the World

THE THEATRICAL DESIGNS OF TANYA MOISEIWITSCH

ORGANIZED BY

T. J. EDELSTEIN

WITH ESSAYS BY

ALAN BARLOW

DENNIS BEHL

ROBERTSON DAVIES

T. J. EDELSTEIN

THE DAVID AND ALFRED SMART MUSEUM OF ART

THE UNIVERSITY OF CHICAGO

IN ASSOCIATION WITH

THE UNIVERSITY OF WASHINGTON PRESS

For Elliott Hayes

This catalogue accompanies the exhibition *The Stage Is All the World: The Theatrical Designs of Tanya Moiseiwitsch*, organized by the David and Alfred Smart Museum of Art, the University of Chicago; The Stratford Shakespearean Festival Foundation of Canada; and Parnassus Foundation; and presented at the following institutions:

David and Alfred Smart Museum of Art,
University of Chicago
14 April–12 June 1994

Mira Godard Gallery, Toronto
12 July–27 August 1994

Frederick R. Weisman Art Museum at the
University of Minnesota, Minneapolis
29 September–4 December 1994

Marion Koogler McNay Art Museum,
San Antonio
26 March–25 June 1995

David and Alfred Smart Museum of Art
University of Chicago
5550 S. Greenwood Ave.
Chicago, Ill. 60637   U.S.A.
telephone (312) 702-0200   fax (312) 702-3121

Frontispiece: Lee Richardson as Apollo and Len Cariou as Orestes in *The House of Atreus*, Guthrie Theater, Minneapolis, 1967 (photo: Don Getsug Studios)

Page v: Tanya Moiseiwitsch at the Abbey Theatre, Dublin, 1938 (photo: Courtesy of the Stratford Festival, Canada. Photographer unknown)

Page vii: Michael Bates as Bardolph and Anthony Quayle as Falstaff in act 4, scene 2 of *Henry IV, Part I*, Shakespeare Memorial Theatre, Stratford-upon-Avon, 1951 (photo: Angus McBean. Harvard Theatre Collection)

Produced by Stephanie D'Alessandro

Designed by Joan Sommers Design, Chicago

Photography by Jerry Kobylecky Museum Photography
  (unless otherwise noted)

Printed by The Stinehour Press on Mohawk Superfine

Text set in Sabon roman, Display in Linoscript and Franklin Gothic

Cover photograph: © Matthew Gilson, 1994

Library of Congress Catalogue Card Number 93-85974
ISBN 0-935573-14-3

This catalogue is printed on acid-free paper.

Tanya —
Abbey Theatre

Contents

Prologue: The Stage Is All the World

THE TITLE WE HAVE CHOSEN for this retrospective exhibition of the work of Tanya Moiseiwitsch is, we think, a fitting one. The expression was used in a lecture delivered in July 1985 by the late distinguished literary scholar Northrop Frye at the Festival Theatre in Stratford, Ontario. Frye noted that Shakespeare's Globe Theatre bore a Latin motto which translates as "Nearly all the world's a stage." With his typical acerbic wit, Frye observed that only an academician or a lawyer would concern himself with qualifying Shakespeare's "the whole world's a stage" by adding "nearly." "How every fool can play upon the word," Shakespeare might respond to the pedants, for no matter how it is rendered, the essence of the phrase remains the same: there is a powerful link between the theater and our daily lives. We perform our "roles," "mask" our feelings, and develop our "personae," employing the terms which come to us from the dramatic art of classical antiquity to describe our behavior. For millennia, we have seen the stage as a metaphor for the world we live in, examining each successive age through the achievements of its artists.

This exhibition celebrates the career of the legendary designer Tanya Moiseiwitsch, who changed the theatrical world for generations to come. She did so by creating the thrust stages at the Stratford Festival in Canada and at the Guthrie Theater in the United States, the first wholly successful thrust stages to be built since the early seventeenth century. Working in association with Tyrone Guthrie, Moiseiwitsch radically and permanently altered the twentieth-century approach to the production of classical plays. By sculpting theatrical space in a way that emphasized the actors' relationship to each other and to the audience, she sharpened the focus on the text. Influenced by the Globe and, perhaps, by its motto, her innovative stage architecture and three-dimensional design concepts inspired a fresh understanding of the classics. The actor-audience relationship she created had the effect of breaking through the "picture frame" of the proscenium arch and its attendant tradition of melodramatic virtuosity. And so we see Moiseiwitsch as an important contributor not only to the contemporary theater but ultimately to the resurgence and broadening of interest in the study of Shakespeare and the classics.

Many individuals have worked enthusiastically and diligently to help make this comprehensive exhibition a success. For their unwavering commitment, we wish to thank the Stratford Festival's former and current artistic directors, David William (1990–93) and Richard Monette, who have enriched our heritage through their masterly use of one of Moiseiwitsch's great architectural settings. We wish to acknowledge Stratford's archivist, Lisa Brant, and, at the University of Chicago, associate curator Stephanie D'Alessandro of the David and Alfred Smart Museum of Art, and thank them for their important work in bringing this project to fruition. We are especially grateful to Teri Edelstein, Deputy Director of the Art Institute of Chicago, who in her former capacity as director of the Smart Museum and as curator of the exhibition, recognized the importance of Moiseiwitsch's work and made this project possible by generously providing her scholarship and experience.

The exhibition and the essays that follow explore the many facets of Moiseiwitsch's design artistry. By honoring her, we also pay special tribute to the crucial contribution she made to the formation and evolution of the living theatrical tradition, now in its fifth decade, at the Stratford Festival in Canada.

RAPHAEL BERNSTEIN
President
Parnassus Foundation

RICHARD A. BORN
Acting Director and Curator
David and Alfred Smart Museum of Art
University of Chicago

ELLIOTT HAYES
Literary Manager
Stratford Festival

Acknowledgments

SHORTLY AFTER COMING TO THE SMART MUSEUM as director in 1990, I was invited by Raphael Bernstein of the Parnassus Foundation to organize a retrospective of the work of Tanya Moiseiwitsch in association with the Foundation and the Stratford Festival. A spirit of cooperation and creativity has characterized this enterprise from the beginning, and I am exceedingly grateful for it. Raph Bernstein provided invaluable support and friendship, and helped me develop other relationships essential to the project, not surprisingly because they are with invaluable people. Most important among these is the artist herself, and it will not seem hyperbole to anyone who knows Tanya Moiseiwitsch to say that her extraordinary talent and influence are matched by her warmth, intelligence, and generosity. She has enabled this project through her creative achievement, by graciously sharing all materials and information, and through her many friends and associates, who responded with admiration and devotion to the myriad needs of the exhibition and catalogue.

Chief in this category are the staff of the Stratford Festival. Thanks are due in some way to everyone connected with the Festival, but I must distinguish with special gratitude Lisa Brant, Archivist; Ellen Cole, former Director of Communications; Matte Downey, Archives Assistant; Debra Hanson, Head of Design; Robert Ihrig, Exhibitions Co-ordinator; Susan Lemenchick, Administrative Assistant, Director's Office; Richard Monette, Artistic Director; Janice Price, Director of Marketing and Communications; Gary Thomas, General Manager; David William, Artistic Director (1990-93); the board of directors of the Festival, especially Raph Bernstein and Hope Abelson; and most particularly Elliott Hayes, Literary Manager. My association with Stratford has been marked by unequalled professionalism and pleasure.

The same can be said of the entire staff of the Smart Museum, who handled the details of a complex international loan exhibition: Rudy Bernal, Chief Preparator; Richard A. Born, Acting Director and Curator; Stephanie D'Alessandro, Associate Curator; Kathleen Gibbons, Education Director; Ken Kocanda, Registrarial

Intern; Bruce Linn, Registrar; Christopher Marhefka, Security Supervisor; Craig Newsom, Preparatorial Intern; Jessica Rose, Administrative Assistant; Rachel Rosenberg, former Public Information Officer/Membership Coordinator; Britt Salvesen, former Curatorial Intern; Elizabeth Siegel, Curatorial Intern; Priscilla Stratten, Operations Manager; and Gavin Witt, former Development Intern. My appreciation to all of them, and to Jerry Kobylecky, Museum Photography, and Joan Sommers Design, Chicago, for their very professional work on the catalogue. Additionally, for programing at the Court Theatre at the University of Chicago in conjunction with the Moiseiwitsch exhibition, we are grateful to Sandy Bateman, Managing Director; Rebecca Manery, Education Director; Charles Newell, Associate Artistic Director; Jodi Royce, Marketing Director; and Nicholas Rudall, Executive Director.

This project would not have been possible without Robertson Davies, Alan Barlow, and Dennis Behl, who wrote the catalogue, and Dirk Campbell and Mikal Miller, Dirk Productions, Ltd., who helped bring the designs alive through video. Tanya's contributions would not be known to this audience without their efforts. The lenders to the exhibition, listed separately in this catalogue, contributed not only objects but also research and expertise. In this regard, thanks are owed to the staff of the Theatre Museum, London, including Margaret Benton, Head of Museum; James Fowler, Deputy Head of Museum; Andrew Kirk, Curatorial Assistant; Leela Meinertas, Registrar; Barry Norman, Curatorial Assistant; and Sarah Woodcock, Research Assistant. We are grateful to those at the Guthrie Theater, Minneapolis, who also provided valuable assistance: Teresa Eyring, Assistant Executive Director; Amy Forton, Public Relations Director; Annette Garceau, Costume Shop; Edward A. Martenson, Executive Director; and Lara Rindfleisch, Public Relations Assistant. For research and loans from the Guthrie Theater Archives, University of Minnesota Libraries, St. Paul, our thanks to Barbara Bezat, Assistant to the Curator, and Professor Alan Lathrop, Curator and Director. Similarly, acknowledgment is due Jennifer Aylmer, who was so helpful with loans from Tanya's collection, as well as Jeanne T. Newlin, Curator, Harvard Theatre Collection, Cambridge, Mass.; Marion Pringle, Senior Librarian, Shakespeare Centre Library, Stratford-upon-Avon; Roger Pringle, Director, Shakespeare Birthplace Trust, Stratford-upon-Avon; Norma Campbell Vickers, John Vickers Theatre Collection, London; Rowena Willard, Loans Officer at the Victoria and Albert Museum, London, and the Picture Library of the museum.

My thanks also to our collaborators at the other exhibition venues: Lyndel King, Director, and Patricia McDonnell, Curator, at the Frederick R. Weisman Art Museum at the University of Minnesota, Minneapolis; William Chiego, Director, and Linda M. Hardberger, Curator, Tobin Collection, at the Marion Koogler McNay Art Museum, San Antonio; and Mira Godard, Director, Mira Godard Gallery, Toronto. Others who have aided in crucial ways to research, organize, and present this exhibition include James Bakkom; Carlo Catenazzi, Head Photographer, Art Gallery of Ontario; Rob Freeman, Director/Curator, Gallery/Stratford; Don Getsug, Don Getsug Studios; Mr. and Mrs. F. Desmond Hall; Dr. Raymond Ingram; Jeanette Neal, Executive Director, Parnassus Foundation; Chris Conniff-O'Shea, Department Specialist, and Harriet Stratis, Associate Conservator of Prints and Drawings, at the Art Institute of Chicago.

The theater is a complex and collaborative medium, and just as this exhibition echoes Tanya's monumental contribution to the theater its collaborative nature recalls the herculean task of putting on a play. It is a great privilege for me to have been given the opportunity to make Tanya Moiseiwitsch's achievements available to a larger group of people and to coordinate the efforts of so many who joined with me in making these accomplishments known. To all of them, whether mentioned by name or not, I extend my most profound gratitude.

T. J. EDELSTEIN

Lenders to the Exhibition

James and Gail Bakkom, Minneapolis

Mrs. A. M. Bell, Stratford, Ontario

Dirk Campbell, London

Moira Wylie, Toronto

Gallery/Stratford, Stratford, Ontario

Annette Garceau, Minneapolis

Guthrie Theater, Minneapolis

Guthrie Theater Archives, University of Minnesota Libraries, St. Paul

Tanya Moiseiwitsch, London

Private collection

Shakespeare Centre Library, Stratford-upon-Avon

The Stratford Festival, Ontario

The Theatre Museum, London

Note to the Reader

UNLESS OTHERWISE NOTED, all quotes from Tanya Moiseiwitsch in the following essays are derived from interviews with the artist conducted by Alan Barlow and Elliott Hayes on 27 and 28 February and in March 1991. For the sake of consistency, the American spelling of words such as "center," "color," and "theater" has been used instead of the British spelling, except in the formal names of institutions.

The checklist sections represent designs by Moiseiwitsch included in the exhibition; catalogue numbers refer to the objects listed in these sections. Within each production, objects are listed by category in the following order: research books, set designs and models, costume sketches, property sketches, and actual costumes and masks. In instances of multiple works from one production, theater, date, and director are given under the first listing for each production; where known, names of actors and actresses are listed after the first appearance of the character. Titles are based on notations on the works. Dimensions are in inches followed by centimeters in parentheses; height precedes width precedes depth. For works on paper, dimensions are for sheet sizes unless otherwise indicated. Objects not illustrated in the catalogue are noted by an asterisk.

ROBERTSON DAVIES

Tanya Moiseiwitsch:
An Appreciation

CYNICS ARE WRONG WHO SAY that wishes, when granted, invariably prove disappointing. I was nineteen when first I saw Tanya Moiseiwitsch and longed to talk to her, and thirty-nine when at last I did so. It was anything but a disappointment, and has indeed been a delight ever since. Our first encounter was in Malvern, England at the 1932 summer festival of unusual and new plays offered by Sir Barry Jackson. I was there because my parents wished to indulge my love for the theater, and I was being edified by one of Sir Barry's chronologically designed seasons. Not only great classics like Ben Jonson's *Alchemist*, but also rarities like Nicholas Udall's *Ralph Roister Doister* and Thomas Southerne's *Oroonoko* were deployed before my astonished eyes. But one did not, of course, spend all day in the theater; one walked in the beautiful public gardens, and it was there I saw the fascinating girl I later learned was Tanya Moiseiwitsch.

I wanted to make her acquaintance, but that was out of the question. One saw all sorts of notable people in the gardens, taking the air. Many of them were the stars of the theater—Ralph Richardson, who had the lead in *Oroonoko* and the role of Face in the Jonson; Ernest Thesiger, performing Ralph Roister Doister, and Dazzle in Dion Boucicault's *London Assurance*; and Cedric Hardwicke, brilliant as Abel Drugger in *The Alchemist*. But the cynosure of all eyes was the group surrounding George Bernard Shaw and his wife: Sir Barry himself; John Drinkwater, the poet and playwright; his wife, Daisy Kennedy, the Australian violinist;

and, standing modestly a pace or two behind these great ones, Kennedy's daughter—the amazing girl.

Amazing because of the fixity and solemnity of her expression, as if she were listening to something beyond the fireworks of Shaw, who seemed to do all the talking. Amazing also because of the beauty of her eyes, large and dark like those one sees in Russian icons. A girl obviously far and away above the girls I knew, who were pleasant enough but giggled and chattered and never seemed to see or hear anything very interesting. There was no question of approaching her.

So I stared, and wished. And at last I met Tanya, when she came to Canada in 1953. I was a member of the board of the Stratford Festival Theatre in Ontario during the first twenty years of its life, and my wife and I were personal friends of the director Sir Tyrone Guthrie and of Lady Guthrie. They asked us to go to Stratford while the theater was still under construction to see what was being done, and it was there that we met Tanya, who was supervising the building of the thrust stage she had designed, and which is still in use today.

Tanya was the daughter of her mother's first husband, the pianist Benno Moiseiwitsch. With the passing of years, this seems to me increasingly important, for he was a great artist and wit, and so is Tanya. Benno Moiseiwitsch was, until his death in 1963, one of the most accomplished pianists of his day, and of a distinguished musical line: he was a pupil of the mighty Théodore

Leschetitzsky, maker of many artists of the first rank and himself a pupil of Carl Czerny, whose teacher had been Beethoven. Benno—if I may be excused that familiarity in writing of a man with a long name—was renowned for his soaring approach to music, governed by elegant taste and a superb technique. He was, critics agreed, primarily a lyric player of unusual fluency and subtlety, extraordinary in the romantic repertoire from Chopin to Rachmaninoff (who declared him to be his artistic heir) and of an impeccable musicality. A romantic firmly grounded in the classics, as is his daughter.

Tanya tells of playing piano for her father when she was a child. He gave her a big hug, then declared, "But that's not for your playing, darling." Her art, it is true, was to lie in another direction. Her wit, however, may well be like her father's, which was, as his friend James Agate claimed, catlike—not wounding but playful and ambiguously caressing. Agate recalled an evening at the Savage Club in London, where he and Benno were habitués, when Agate said, "Mark is playing in Edinburgh tonight." Mark was pianist Mark Hambourg, another club member and bridge companion of both men. "If someone would open a window," mused Benno, "perhaps we could hear him." Indeed, Hambourg's playing could descend embarrassingly from heaven-storming greatness to mere rowdiness, and he had a fine disregard for wrong notes. His presence accorded with his artistry. Tanya remembers being brought from her bed as a small child to meet Mark; she stood at the top of the stair gazing down on the corpulent man, wild of hair and thick of spectacles, like Beethoven seen in a distorting mirror. "What is it?" she cried in fright, and rushed back into the nursery.

This was her childhood, a world of musicians, poets, theater folk, but none of them, so far as I know, painters. It was her stepfather, John Drinkwater, who urged her in the direction of the theater. His influence on the speaking of Shakespearean verse was manifest for many years in the outdoor productions in Regent's Park in London. As a schoolboy, I listened many times to the lecture "On the Speaking of Verse," which he had recorded for the guidance of just such hearers as I. Drinkwater's taste was flawless, but never precious, his feeling for rhythm as refined as that of any musician. His pronunciation seemed to hark back through that of Sir Johnston Forbes-Robertson to the beginning of the nineteenth century, before the coming of that accent, now almost past, which was called "English" but was really the speech of a rather small group. Drinkwater introduced Tanya to the practical work of backstage and the scene-dock, where she learned the realities of her craft that underlie all her splendid inventions.

She would not call herself a painter. She denies that she can draw. But she is contradicted by the grace of her line and a sense of color that has not been approached by any other designer. These things did not come at once, but after a long apprenticeship at the Abbey Theatre in Dublin, at The Oxford Playhouse, the Old Vic, and the Memorial Theatre at Stratford-upon-Avon. It is stupid to speak of an artist's name "being made" by a single work, but her designs for *Henry VIII* at Stratford in 1949 attracted very serious attention. Her work became associated with that of the great Guthrie. It was as though his own strong, but not sophisticated, visual sense found its outlet in greatly enlarged form in Tanya's designs for many of his finest productions. Nor was she simply a canvas-and-paint designer; the permanent setting at the Stratford Festival Theatre tells all that need be told of her fine architectural sense, and it will stand in the history of theater as a new concept, rooted, as always in Tanya's work, in a deep understanding of the past and a feeling for materials.

Materials, and craftsmanship. She once came upon my eldest daughter sewing costumes for a Stratford production (the students were expected to help where they could) and she observed that Miranda was "felling" a seam. "It's been a long time since I've seen anyone do that," she said, in a tone that, to a student, was an accolade. Tanya has worked in poor theaters, where it is necessary to look at both sides of a penny, so she knows the value of economy, but never the economy of bad work or second best. When she came to Stratford in Canada, she astonished the management by insisting on genuine materials—real leather, real silks and wools, palpable things which, as she put it, "once had lived." What this means is apparent in any play that she designs and dresses; her work has a reality, a depth, which is directly opposite to the common meaning of "theatrical."

Not, of course, that she is lacking in theatrical expertise. There is not a trick of the trade she does not know. Her decoration of the chapel in Massey College in the University of Toronto, perhaps her only non-theatrical venture in establishing an atmosphere, is a case in point. The architect had created large panels in the walls, composed of rounded pebbles stuck in plaster and painted a dark red, which proved, when completed, to be too aggressive a color. What was to be done? "Paint them with butter-milk," said Tanya, and it was done, producing just the right effect. And in the course of time, the pungent smell, which would not have caused much comment in a scene-painter's atelier, disappeared.

This exhibition gives much, but cannot give all, of the quality of her work, because it is immobile and her costumes are all intended to be seen in movement and in changing effects of color as they encounter one another on the stage. But if you look imaginatively, you will observe much of what makes all the plays Tanya Moiseiwitsch has designed as truly dramatic as the acting: her work is never obtrusive, but seamlessly integrated with that of all the other theater artists. These are the robes of Thespis, freshly imagined for every play, by the inheritor of a great tradition of strength governed by impeccable taste.

ALAN BARLOW

Tanya Moiseiwitsch and the Work of the Stage Designer

"SETTINGS AND COSTUMES DESIGNED BY..." The average theatergoer glances at these words in the program, has a momentary image of a shadowy figure backstage who "paints scenery" or "draws what the clothes should look like," and imagines, perhaps, that this is the sum total of the designer's contributions to the evening's entertainment.

In fact, the work of the professional stage designer is complex and all-demanding. He or she is concerned with every aspect of the *visual* side of the stage presentation. Usually the designer does not "paint scenery"—that is the job of the scene painter working from the painted scale model provided by the designer, but, of course, the designer has to know the techniques involved. Tanya Moiseiwitsch first learned these as a scene-painting student on the paint frame of the famous Old Vic Theatre, London, in 1933, a time when Tyrone Guthrie, with whom she was later to collaborate so memorably, was directing his first season there. They would meet professionally and sometimes socially, but the days of their famous alliance were still far off. Tanya's experience in scene painting, which included falling off a ladder into a bucket of paint and breaking her arm, was to continue for the next ten years, while she designed, as well as painted, settings for the Abbey Theatre, Dublin; the Q Theatre, London; and the Playhouse, Oxford.

But it is not only the designing and the painting of the scenery which is the designer's concern. Ground plans and working drawings have to be made; he or she must oversee the making of the setting, choose the canvases, metals, plastics, woods for its con-struction; the colors, pigments, stains, dyes for its painting; the techniques used in their application. Sometimes furniture has to be designed: vehicles, monsters, moving machinery. Drawings for each costume have to be produced; fabrics, braids, buttons, linings, decoration to be chosen; pattern and cut to be decided; attention paid to period detail, accuracy, and research; jewelry, shoes, boots, scarves, belts, shawls, gloves, fans, fobs, furs, and furbelows must be designed or selected; sometimes costumes, once made, have to be "broken down"—that is, burnt, torn, splashed with dye or bleach or paint to make them look worn, sweaty, ragged. Wigs, false hair, bald pates, eyebrows, moustaches, beards, paddings for the human frame to look older, or younger, or more voluptuous, or more obese (a subtle art), or grotesque, or like an animal. Face makeup, body makeup, masks—all these can be part of the designer's everyday job. The designer is also concerned with what the man in the front row of the stalls sees, and the man in the back row of the gallery does not see, of the stage. It is the designer who chooses or designs the stage properties (that is, of course, everything handled by the actors on stage), who chooses color and texture, and judges the effect of lighting on these; is concerned with the colors of the lighting, also its angles, directions, and "moods." It is the designer who, most often with an assistant, makes elaborately detailed scale models and endless lists; deals with nervous actors, demanding directors, overworked staffs; attends wig-fittings, show-fittings; works to constricting budgets and construction schedules. In fact, the designer's life, as the first night draws near, is a complexity of diverse threads held together by a single vision, a vision ultimately to be summarized by the words: "settings and costumes by...."

Stage design, then, is not merely a matter of producing drawings and paintings such as those seen in this exhibition. Drawings do have to be produced, otherwise designers have no means of showing their ideas to the director and workshops backstage, but however pleasant these may be as pictures, they are not, in the first place, an end in themselves. A good stage designer does not necessarily have to draw well, for the job is to "paint," as it were, in three dimensions, with the environment being provided for the actors, with the changes of stage lighting, with the movement and flow of colors and costume, with the living change and bustle of the stage performance.

Tanya, with typical modesty, has always insisted that she cannot draw. Many are the times I have heard her say, "Oh if I only could get the drawing right! Just look at those *hands*! What *do* they look like!" But of course it was never the hands, however well they were drawn (which they often were), that mattered: it was the sleeve from which the hands emerged, the costume as a whole, her innate instinct for period, character, silhouette, the sensitive theatricality, and the *rightness* of it all that mattered. Guthrie once said to her, "You really are the worst draw-er in the business, but I can see what you mean," and harsh as that judgement undoubtedly was, the communication of the idea to the director was certainly there, and that, for the designer, ultimately is all that really matters.

How does the designer set about designing the stage picture? First of all, of course, there is the script to be read, and to be read not once but many, many times, and read with a critical and above all an *analytical* eye, searching for every reference, however oblique, to the visual requirements of the text. Notes must be made of the kind of research that is needed—period research, architecture, artifacts, costumes, furniture, interior decoration; geographical research; technical research. The designer looks for clues to the psychology of every character, and through them to

the kind of setting they will make for themselves or in which they find themselves; for the kind of give aways each character will display, consciously or unconsciously, in their choice (or non-choice) of the clothes they wear; for clues to climate and season; to mood, style, atmosphere, symbolism, color.

At some time in this earliest of stages the designer must meet the director. On the close collaboration of these two so much depends. "It was Hugh Hunt at the Abbey Theatre Dublin," Tanya says, again with her characteristic modesty, "who first gave me the idea that the director must always have first say in what is wanted; the shape of the play, the look of the play; the atmosphere to be created; even where the furniture would go, where doors and windows would be most appropriate—all these details which are so important to the designer, particularly if it is a realistic play.... There *are* designers who are able to come up with the first idea; I just don't belong to that category—it's too much responsibility, too daunting when the director comes up with a better one and yours is cast out. I'd rather be the one who follows and as closely as possible tries to express what the director is aiming at, what the author was aiming at when he wrote the play.... If Guthrie—or another director—came up with an idea which I could not go along with, *he* would make it clear to me by telling it to me another way and then I would say, 'Oh, I see what you mean,' and he would say, 'So long as you *do*, but if you don't for goodness sake say so NOW.' He would listen, I admit he would listen, and I think he would say to himself, 'She needs a new version of this idea; I'll work out something and see if I can persuade her this way.' He certainly did that and it was fairly transparent and I fell for it every time because I did see on second or third try exactly what he meant, and then I *did* go along with it because by then I understood it."

The relationship between director and designer is not always like this. Some directors come to the first meeting with very positive, even rigid ideas; others want the designer to present them with virtually a *fait accompli*. Between these two extremes (and most designers have known them both) there are many variations.

But whatever the relationship, the designer needs, as Tanya is fond of saying, "to get inside the director's thinking box, to do what *they* could have done themselves if they'd been able to draw and paint."

One of the initial headaches at this stage may be the settling of scene changes. Often the designer has to think of *rapid* scene change, and his or her ingenuity may be taxed to the utmost to devise ways in which, say, an exterior may become an elaborately furnished interior, and vice versa, in a matter, literally, of seconds. To hold up the action for a lengthy scene change may well be disastrous to the dramatic flow of the play. When, in 1944, Tyrone Guthrie first saw a production designed by Tanya—a *Merchant of Venice* at the Playhouse, Oxford—he pronounced it "too uppy-downy," by which he meant that the curtain kept coming down to facilitate a scene change. "I hadn't been taught at that point," Tanya comments, "that Shakespeare should just keep rolling along without the scenery holding up the action, so it was, indeed, *very* 'uppy-downy,' and I remembered the phrase over the years, and of course, when we worked together we got away from all that." In spite of his criticism, Guthrie then and there invited Tanya to Liverpool, where he was running a three-weekly repertory company, and it was there, as a result of the "uppy-downy" *Merchant of Venice*, that their now historic collaboration first began.

Tanya was still a long way from the strong, permanent set she designed for *Henry VIII* at Stratford, England, in 1949, which I heard one director at that time describe as "a set I would be prepared to direct *any* Shakespeare play in," still further from the 1951 permanent setting for four history plays at the same theater, and from the invention of the Stratford, Ontario stage which has, indeed, seen all the plays of Shakespeare played on its brilliant arrangement of rostra and balcony, but she had now learned that the designer must not only design the stage as seen by the audience, but also (if there are to be many scene changes) the stage as used by the scene-changing staff. Only on a to-scale ground plan of the stage (provided at the onset by the theater management) can the designer, with the help of the technical director, work out the placing of each setting, and determine how much room is available at any point backstage for storage and for movement. The designer's final ground plans will have solved many problems, and will also show how the scenery is to be "broken up" into its various components such as flats, cloths, ground-rows, etc.

With the ground plans more or less settled, the designer's next move is to make a scale model of all the settings. Often this is done with an assistant. By means of the model not only the scene changes, but also problems of carpentry, of color, of lighting, of stage movement, of masking off the backstage areas, can be solved in detail. Any important property such as a bale of straw, a fishing net, a sea monster, or a stagecoach, is made in model form also, for the director to see in position on the scaled-down stage. From the component parts of the model, working drawings for each piece of scenery are made, and once these are constructed and sent to the paint shops, the model passes into the hands of the scene painters to be their guide in the painting of the setting. The stage designer must be at hand to answer all queries.

At quite an early stage in the production schedule, the designer receives a complete cast list from the director. With it, and preferably with some knowledge of each actor's physique, the designs appear in rapid succession. In doing them, the designer thinks not only of the character as seen by the author and director, but also of the actor's body shape and how, if necessary, it may be changed to be more in keeping with the part in question. Each costume is related in color and texture to those with which it will be seen at every moment of the play's progression, related, too, to the scenic background already designed. The appropriate fabrics and cut of the costume are in the designer's mind as the drawing proceeds. "One must draw *already*," Tanya says, "not necessarily in order to produce a work of art (which, frankly, I don't think I am capable of doing) but to produce a *working* drawing from which the costume makers, wig makers, boot makers, jewelry makers—all those people who contribute can *read* what you are asking for and translate it into reality. The comfort and well-being of the actor is of paramount importance. Comfort is rather a loose term; sometimes one has to bend it if they *need* to be encumbered with heavy costumes. But if they *can* bear that, and try to look like your design, so that the director doesn't get a shock when he sees them and says 'that's not in the least like what we planned,' then I think the designer has done the job he or she was asked to do!"

Inevitably, as she says this, one thinks of her designs for *Oedipus* and *The House of Atreus* where the willing actors were subjected to the greatest discomfort in oversize masks and body-paddings which called for a whole new vocabulary of movement and gesture. These designs were, in the first place, inspired by Guthrie's vision of the plays in terms of a ritual of cosmic dimensions, and as a result of his prompting her to greater and greater exaggeration, she came to be in awe of the scale she had created. Her gratitude to the actors and her admiration for their lack of complaint still know no bounds.

The actors do not, as a general rule, see the designs until everyone is assembled for the first reading of the play. At this meeting the director will give a more or less brief account of his views in approaching the play, questions will be asked by the players, usually connected with some point of interpretation of their own roles, and then the designer may talk about the settings and show the model and costume designs. Occasionally, in discussion with the actors, new aspects of a particular character, and therefore the costume, may emerge which have not previously been considered and another design produced along new lines.

After this "launching" the designer's job is a constant round of visits to carpenters, prop shops, wardrobe, fitting-rooms, wig-makers, paint shops, etc., rehearsals, production-meetings, the publicity department, museums, libraries, department stores, junk shops, and more production-meetings, and since, particularly with big shows, many of these appointments will overlap, he or she must have a well-trained assistant to help shoulder the burden.

Once everything has been completed under his or her supervision, the dress rehearsals find the designer in the empty, darkened amphitheater, scrutinizing the stage with a hawk-eye, and jotting down such notes as: "Two extra petticoats for C.," "J. having difficulty with O.P. stairs," "G.R. battens too close to eye," "Y's tights wrinkled at the knee," "M's tights not wrinkled enough," "Is that D.L. wing braced properly?," "Can see batten 3 from front row of stalls," "Amber gel. killing M's bodice; change to straw??," "Take 1/4 inch off L's cuffs," etc., until all the problems, hopefully, have been solved and the first night comes not only as a climactic sharing with the audience of months of work, but also a relief and a release, for from there on the designer's job is over, and the show is in other, maintenance, hands.

When I first showed Tanya these descriptions of a designer's work she said, "You make it all sound like *jolly hard work*!," and then, in a tone of surprise bordering on one of self-discovery, she added, "But then, I *suppose* it is!" That comment was a clue to Tanya's total, loving absorption in the craft of theater. Perhaps it will never be possible to assess fully Tanya's quiet but so far-reaching influence on twentieth-century theater; an influence which spreads beyond the visual aspects of design to all kinds of backstage ways of working, and, of course, to the complete revision of our ideas about the relationship of stage to audience. Guthrie's criticism of the "uppy-downy" *Merchant of Venice* was ultimately, through Tanya, to see a universal breakaway from the confinements of the proscenium stage to an actor/audience relationship which gave new life and vision to directors and designers throughout the world.

As has been seen, the work of the stage designer is nothing if not one of collaboration with others. It was this which first attracted Tanya to the job, and it has been her firm adherence to the highest standards within those collaborations, coupled with her constant readiness to learn from others, that has made her so well loved in all the many theaters in which she has worked.

Michael Gwynn as the Duke of York, Alexander Gauge as the Earl of Northumberland, and Hugh Griffith as John of Gaunt in act 3, scene 5 of *Richard II*, Shakespeare Memorial Theatre, Stratford-upon-Avon, 1951 (photo: Angus McBean. Harvard Theatre Collection)

T. J. EDELSTEIN

Visualizing Drama

IN THE COSTUME WORKSHOPS of the Stratford Festival Theatre in Ontario, one's senses are dazzled—by bolts of bright cloth; piles of braid, beads, and buttons; swiftly moving hands and bodies; a hum of conversation and machines; and the slightly surreal, immobile population of headless torsos which are the dressmakers' dummies. There is a sensation, too, of butterflies fluttering about one's head, as colorful cloth swatches affixed to drawings on paper move with the currents of air. These drawings, with their attached fabric samples, hang above the heads of the cutters and seamstresses for easy reference. From the figures rendered on these sheets, supplemented by consultations and fittings, the extraordinary costumes we see on the stage are produced. The costumes are, in turn, brought to life by the bodies, movements, and voices of the actors.

When we view the designs by Tanya Moiseiwitsch in this exhibition, it is important to remember their original, functional context, for these images were made to direct the hands of craftsmen and -women who translated their abstract shapes into palpable reality. Their mute instruction has led to sets, costumes, and props. If they were meant to be hung on a wall, it was the wall of the workroom, not the museum. But Moiseiwitsch's talent is such that her drawings are often much more than visual aids. Although she denies, with a modesty bordering on self-effacement, the "artistic" validity of her drawings, they often give the lie to her protestations. Created in the flurry of a production schedule, they frequently do bear evidence of hurried execution, and because they serve as guides in the workroom, figures often seem stiff, with elegant composition giving way to a detailed description of a ruffle or a sleeve. And yet, many of the drawings have an extraor-

dinary power beyond their utilitarian nature; they repay our viewing as documents of the theater, as traces of an exciting collaborative process, and as truly aesthetic objects.

For those of us not fortunate to have seen them realized on stage, moreover, these designs can suggest the visual delights of some of the most successful theatrical productions of this century. The exhibition surveys the chronological framework of Moiseiwitsch's career, which spans more than five decades. A set design for *Uncle Vanya* at the Old Vic in London in 1945 (fig. no. 1, color plate 2) is juxtaposed with a costume sketch for Michael Bryant as Sir Paul Plyant in *The Double Dealer* at the National Theatre in 1978 (fig. no. 2). Sketches for sets, costumes, and props, preparatory studies from art and nature, as well as models for sets, costume bibles, and constructed props indicate the varieties of thought and invention needed for a production. Designs for classics of drama—Shakespeare, Ben Jonson, Molière (fig. no. 3, color plate 3)—stand alongside those for operas such as Benjamin Britten's *Peter Grimes* or Antony Hopkins's *Lady Rohesia* (fig. no. 4), to demonstrate the breadth of Moiseiwitsch's experience and vision.

Even in this tiny selection from the more than two hundred productions she has designed, one is struck by the range of her historical sources. An informal sketch of hats for *Romeo and Juliet* at Stratford, Ontario, in 1960 (fig. no. 5), for example, is a veritable catalogue of Italian renaissance male headgear worthy of a Gonzaga or a Medici. Moiseiwitsch recalls how Tyrone Guthrie, during their famous collaboration, encouraged her research in art history: "He and many other directors I've worked with had a keen visual sense and sometimes called on various well-known or

1. *Set Design, Act 1* from *Uncle Vanya*, 1945, cat. no. 1

2. *Sir Paul Plyant* from *The Double Dealer*, 1978, cat. no. 19

3. *Set Model* from *Tartuffe*, 1983–84, cat. no. 21

1

2

3

4. *Set Design, Scene* 2 from *Lady Rohesia*, 1948, cat. no. 3

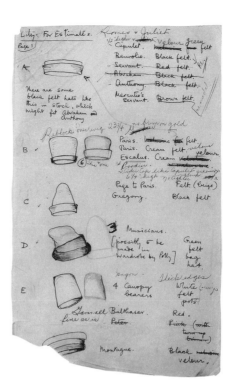

5. *Sketches of Hats* from *Romeo and Juliet*, 1960, cat. no. 11

6. *Research Designs after Adriaen van Ostade and Franz Hals* from *The Merry Wives of Windsor*, 1956, cat. no. 9

lesser-known painters for me to look at and get ideas from—not slavishly to copy but to be inspired by." Indeed, Moiseiwitsch's notebooks are filled with sketches from paintings, prints, and drawings by an extraordinary number of artists. "On occasion," she observes, "I have leaned very heavily on a particular painter, and though that might not be visible to the audience, certainly for me it was a wonderful prop in the business of designing the sets and costumes." Her hours of study in museums, print rooms, and libraries are apparent, not in historicizing minutiae, but in the richness and resonance of her designs, in which, in the tradition of stage design, art-historical references are subtly incorporated and transformed.

Often a painter would provide inspiration not by style but through color. Moiseiwitsch remembers that she and Guthrie once discussed whether a certain production should be in "Van Dyck browns." For *The Merry Wives of Windsor* at Stratford, Ontario, in 1956, she inhabits the world of the Dutch Masters—Gerard Terborch, Jan Steen, and Adriaen van Ostade. In the studies for *Merry Wives* (fig. no. 6), all the details—hats, bodices, sleeves—are rounded. They are homey and comfortable, a dramatic contrast to Moiseiwitsch's designs for a 1964 production of Jonson's *Volpone* at the Guthrie Theater in Minneapolis. For this project,

T.M.
1964

7. *Studies of Birds* from
   Volpone, 1964, cat. no. 12

8. *Voltore* from *Volpone*, 1964,
   cat. no. 13

9. *John of Gaunt, Scenes 1 and 3* from *Richard II*, 1951, cat. no. 54 (photo: Shakespeare Centre Library, Stratford-upon-Avon)

Guthrie advised her to study birds, and her pencil sketches (fig. no. 7) demonstrate that she carried out his directive. The theme of a bird of prey is extremely apt for a play populated with a variety of rapacious, greedy characters. Moiseiwitsch's costume designs brilliantly graft this conceit onto the historically derived clothing and masks of renaissance Venice.

Her Voltore (fig. no. 8, color plate 5), for instance, exhibits the beaky profile and dark "wings" of an avaricious vulture, tempered with the elegant swagger of a Venetian nobleman. In the drawing, the fur trim of Voltore's cape and the hem falling onto the ground are rendered with short brushstrokes which take on the appearance of feathers, the swooping black curve of his hat and pointy beard reinforcing the allusion. Everything in Voltore's costume—hat, nose, chin, shoes—ends in a point, a perfect visualization of the satiric barbs of Jonson's text. Stylistically, Moiseiwitsch's designs have often inspired actors not simply in how their characters should look, but also in the interpretation of their roles. Notations on many of her drawings and notebook pages show how costumes are sometimes keyed to actors' particular movements, or vice versa. An inscription on a drawing for John of Gaunt (fig. no. 9), for instance, from a 1951 production of *Richard II* at the Shakespeare Memorial Theatre (now the Royal Shakespeare Company) in Stratford-upon-Avon, suggests that the character's "coif can be thrown back before prophecy." According to these notes, Moiseiwitsch imagined a "big loose garment to give shrunken appearance inside it" and a "dark grey blanket to huddle over it all & throw back when rising"(see production photograph on page 11).

By the mid-forties, Moiseiwitsch was designing some of the most important productions at the Old Vic in London. An unusual drawing, made for the director Miles Malleson, depicts actors on a set in the "Tilbury scene" of *The Critic* in 1945–46 (fig. no. 10, color plate 1). This production has entered theatrical history because of Laurence Olivier's *tour de force* performances as Sophocles' tragic hero Oedipus followed immediately by Mr. Puff in Richard Brinsley Sheridan's one-act satire. Undoubtedly, Moiseiwitsch's sets enhanced Olivier's acting. Her gay rose-colored rococo setting for *The Critic*, depicted here, is the perfect backdrop for Sheridan's witty play.

10. *Set Design for the Tilbury Scene* from *The Critic or a Tragedy Rehearsed*, 1945–46, cat. no. 2

11. *Fifteen Figures, Scene 8* from *Henry VIII*, 1949, cat. no. 4
(photo: Shakespeare Centre Library, Stratford-upon-Avon)

In 1949, Moiseiwitsch collaborated with Guthrie on a production of *Henry VIII* at the Shakespeare Memorial Theatre. Her designs for this production were inspired by the jewellike Northern renaissance paintings of Hans Holbein. In more than one drawing for Henry, Moiseiwitsch depicts the king with legs planted firmly apart, hands on hips, in the pose made famous by the royal painter. A series of long narrow drawings arrange all the characters in a particular scene on a single sheet (fig. no. 11, color plate 4). Moiseiwitsch explains this unusual format, recalling that Guthrie was in Australia at the time and she needed an easy, compact way to show him the entire color scheme and range of designs she envisioned. The drawings are a wonderful graphic demonstration of how each scene within a production has a palette, a set of hues, indeed, a composition. We can also see how the designer defines a character, or the character's role within a group, by shape and color. Individual costumes then become compositional elements on a stage, and the spatial characteristics of stage and set have a crucial impact on their shifting, three-dimensional relationships.

Moiseiwitsch's brilliant manipulations of three-dimensional space, seen in her stage designs and in the clarity and impact of her costumes (fig. nos. 12, 13, color plate 6), will be her most lasting contribution to theater history. This facility with plastic form is also evident in the props and masks of certain signature productions. The props, for example, for the Stratford Festival's 1985 production of *The Government Inspector* must really be defined as sculpture. Constructed from papier-mâché, gauze, cotton, and paint, the Apparitions of Poverty (fig. no. 14, color plate 7) is powerfully compelling, even when divorced from its original setting and Nikolai Gogol's narrative. The haunting white faces, with their deep-set eyes, huddling together in their misery, loom out of an amorphous mist created by the gauze. They are figures whose substance and form have been drained away. In this work, the drama of the theater can affect us without a stage, lighting, actors, or voices, an apt demonstration of the importance of the designer's art (fig. no. 15).

Executed for the Abbey Theatre, Dublin, in the mid-1930s, Moiseiwitsch's earliest extant costume drawings exhibit a sweet,

12. *Cleopatra's Cloak, Headdress, and Underdress* from *Antony and Cleopatra*, 1967, cat. nos. 14, 15, 16 (photo: Carlo Catenazzi)

13. *Cleopatra's Headdress* from *Antony and Cleopatra*, 1967, cat. no. 15

19

14. *Apparitions of Poverty* from *The Government Inspector*, 1985, cat. no. 22 (photo: Carlo Catenazzi)

5 serfs pulling the Mayor in his turkish bath on wheels.

The Government Inspector.

T.M. '85

15. *Five Serfs Pulling the Mayor in His Turkish Bath on Wheels* from *The Government Inspector*, 1985, cat. no. 23

16. *Neighbors: Men* from *Casadh an t'Súgaín*, 1938, cat. no. 30

17. *Neighbors: Women* from *Casadh an t'Súgaín*, 1938, cat. no. 31

unassuming quality. In two drawings for a 1938 production of Douglas Hyde's *Casadh an t'Súgaín* (*Twisting of the Rope*) (fig. nos. 16, 17, color plates 9, 10), painted in clear bright colors with crisp outlines, figures stand out on the page like a child's cut-out dolls. Four men and four women are portrayed as if linking hands in a dance, their bodies and poses practically interchangeable; only their costumes vary. The vests and jackets on the men create a vertical rhythm of closed and open; the aprons and skirts of the women turn the axis into a horizontal pattern. Although one might be tempted to equate this ingenuousness with the youth and relative inexperience of the designer, it is, rather, evidence of her sophistication. The Abbey Theatre, founded by William Butler Yeats and Lady Augusta Gregory in 1904, was intended to dramatize a native Irish culture. Yeats and his followers recorded folk tales and songs, transforming them into contemporary poetry and theater. The innocent charm of Moiseiwitsch's designs is not naïveté but an homage to the folk sources of the Irish literary movement.

For the 1947 production of *Peter Grimes* at the Royal Opera House, London, Moiseiwitsch adapted historical English dress. Appropriately for provincial England about 1830, the costumes are a combination of early nineteenth-century fashion and occa-

sional late eighteenth-century detail. It is, after all, doubtful that the population of George Crabbe's rural borough—his poem was the literary source for *Peter Grimes*—would have been completely à la mode. Several of Moiseiwitsch's designs bring to mind the work of Richard Redgrave (1804–1888), who specialized in pictures of contemporary life but also in historical subjects. Redgrave illustrated *The Borough* in 1844 for The Etching Club, following the exhibition at the Royal Academy, in 1838, of his *Ellen Orford* (now lost). Orford was another inhabitant of Crabbe's borough and a principal character in *Peter Grimes*. In Redgrave's etching *The False Lover*, she wears a black dress with a white underdress showing at the neck, held by an oval pin, and a white shawl—the exact outfit donned by the character in Moiseiwitsch's designs for the opera (fig. no. 18). Moiseiwitsch's notebooks indicate that the Victoria and Albert Museum, including the National Art Library housed there, was a favorite source for her historical research. Not surprisingly, Redgrave, one of the founders of the museum, is well represented in its collections.

Moiseiwitsch's somber palette for the production is not only historically correct but in keeping with the ominous tone of the story. The image that best epitomizes the narrative, and Britten's music, is a design for a curtain to mask scene changes, a dramatic

21

19. *Design for Interlude Cloth* from *Peter Grimes*, 1947, cat. no. 45 (photo: Collections of the Theatre Museum. By courtesy of the Board of Trustees of the Victoria and Albert Museum, London)

18. *Ellen Orford* from *Peter Grimes*, 1947, cat. no. 47

watercolor in which a small boat is caught in a dark, swirling maelstrom (fig. no. 19, color plate 15). The lines that whirl around the craft are a tangled web of black ink, white pencil, and blue-black wash, with a touch of yellow beneath the ghostly ship. Those familiar with Britten's music will recognize here a visualization of the relentless, interlocking melodies of the score. The unceasing pounding and pitilessness of the sea and, by extension, the inexorable movement of the narrative to its tragic conclusion, are both expressed in this design. The same vortical composition, in which fragile human constructions are surrounded and broken by the movement of nature, is used in the set sketches. Ironically, Moiseiwitsch's powerful curtain design was scrapped after only a few performances because the cloth did not sufficiently muffle the noise of the scene changes. The safety curtain was used instead.

Although Moiseiwitsch demurs when questioned about the possible influence of J. M. W. Turner on the set designs, such a source seems almost certain. The sublime subject of mortal beings dwarfed by nature and the romantic image of the small storm-tossed boat as emblematic of human powerlessness are central to her designs. Such compositions are common in the works of Turner and were surely well known to Moiseiwitsch, an avid museum-goer and well-trained observer. Her watercolor, for instance, is extraordinarily close to the Tate Gallery's 1842 painting titled *Snowstorm—Steam-Boat off a Harbour's Mouth making Signals in Shallow Water, and going by the Lead. The Author was*

22

in this Storm in the Night the Ariel left Harwich. Both the composition and palette of the watercolor are very similar to the Turner painting, Moiseiwitsch even echoing, with the marks of her white pencil, Turner's scumbling of dry white paint across the surface of the canvas. But, appropriately for a design that must be seen from the highest balcony, she further dramatizes the image, strengthening the light/dark contrasts and making the lines of the sea starker and more distinct.

The lines in this drawing express the personality of one of the most important characters in *Peter Grimes*, the sea itself. This embodiment of character through style runs throughout Moiseiwitsch's oeuvre. A drawing for a sweet and pure altar boy contrasted with an evil villainous king makes this point. The Acolyte (fig. no. 20, color plate 15) was designed for *Henry VI, Part I*, one of four *History Plays* produced at the Shakespeare Memorial Theatre in 1951. Moiseiwitsch renders his contours in a smooth, continuous line; the nearly perfect circle of his head and his tiny triangular feet establish an axial plumb line emphasized by the gold curve of his tonsure and the gold band at his neck, on the wrists of his clasped hands, and at the border of his robe. The entire composition is perfectly balanced and perfectly calm, as are, one assumes, his life and soul. Richard III (fig. no. 21, color plate 25), on the other hand, in a drawing for the inaugural production of the Stratford Festival Theatre in 1953, strides asymmetrically across the sheet, as befits his crooked back and corrupt character. The twist of his head and especially of his smile, depicted in blood red, repeated in his undergarment and cloak, express his barbarous venality. Similarly, Queen Margaret (fig. no. 22, color plate 27), in a deep black dress and elongated sleeves with hanging tippets, moves across the page and the stage like an avenging black widow spider.

Most of the productions on which Moiseiwitsch has worked are reinterpretations of classics; most of her designs are carefully grounded in a specific historical period (fig. nos. 23, 24, 25), even when that period is not the original setting of the play. One example is *The Taming of the Shrew* produced at the Stratford Festival in 1954, set not in renaissance Italy but in the American Wild West. The production that many consider her most significant accomplishment is a classic in two senses—as a pillar of European drama and as one of the greatest achievements of the ancient

20. *Acolyte, Scene 14* from *Henry IV, Part I*, 1951, cat. no. 56 (photo: Shakespeare Centre Library, Stratford-upon-Avon)

21. *King Richard III, Scene 15* from *Richard III*, 1953, cat. no. 71

Miss Irene North.   Queen Margaret

Richard III

22. *Queen Margaret* from *Richard III*,
    1953, cat. no. 74

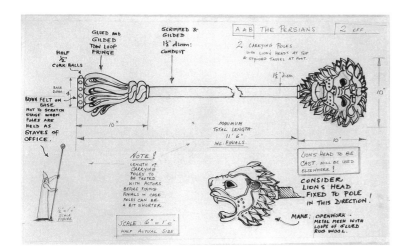

23. *Design for Props* from *The Persians*, 1972, cat. no. 17

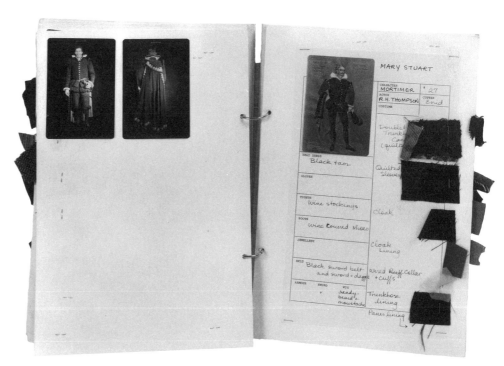

25. "Costume for Mortimer," *Costume Bible* from *Mary Stuart*, 1982, cat. no. 20

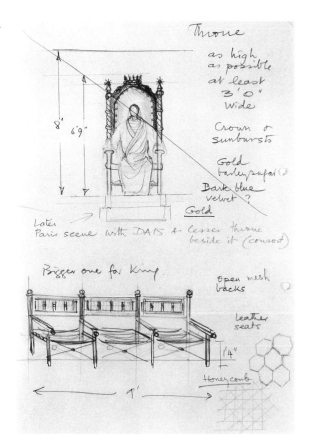

24. "Throne Design," *Research Notebook* from *All's Well That Ends Well*, 1977, cat. no. 18

26

27

28

29

26. "Herakles," *Research Note-book* from *The House of Atreus*, 1967, cat. no. 93

27. "Greek Kouroi," *Research Notebook* from *The House of Atreus*, 1967, cat. no. 93

28. "Leader of the Furies," *Costume Design (Director's Copy)* from *The House of Atreus*, 1967, cat. no. 96 (photo: Guthrie Theater Archives, University of Minnesota Libraries, St. Paul)

29. *Mask Design for the Eumenides* from *The House of Atreus*, 1967, cat. no. 104

world—the *Oresteia* of Aeschylus. In style, her designs for adaptation of the trilogy are uniquely Moiseiwitsch, with synthesized allusions to several historical pasts. Not that she eschewed her usual meticulous study. Her research notebook for what came to be known as *The House of Atreus* at the Guthrie Theater in 1967 is filled with page after page of bold drawings, in ink, pencil, and wash, of masterpieces of the early classical world.

Moiseiwitsch drew the marble Kleobis from Delphi (c. 600–590 B.C.), figures from the Temple of Artemis at Corfu (c. 580 B.C.), a Herakles from the pediment of the Temple of Aphaia Aegina (c. 500–470 B.C.) (fig. no. 26). Over and over, eighteen times in all, she rendered the heads of early Greek kouroi—from the front, side, in three-quarter view—with their ropy, individualized tresses and blank eyes (fig. no. 27). Notations on these pages read "ribbon-like hair," "lion's mane/thick petals," "sun rays," "thick formalised locks." Such sculptures, as well as other monuments in the newspaper and magazine clippings Moiseiwitsch collected in her notebook, all date from around the time of Aeschylus (525–456 B.C.). Her research, however, also included artifacts from the period of the Trojan war, toward the beginning of the twelfth century B.C. From the civilization of Agamemnon, she drew various works of art and, most significantly, pasted a clipping in her notebook of the gold mask said to be of the Mycenaean king himself. Making morphological associations, she added an image of an early gothic stone head discovered at Deganwy Castle in North Wales. Both sculptures display a flattened face with geometricized features—oval eyes, a rectangle nose, and a straight horizontal line for a mouth.

For *The House of Atreus*, Moiseiwitsch put all these carefully observed sources into the crucible of her imagination and created something entirely original. The huge, simplified figures with their broad outlines, the emphatically sculpted masks, a palette limited to the colors of earth and sky, gave the production a primal power. In the actual performance, Aeschylus's drama, Guthrie's staging and direction, and the actors' performances would all wield their force. But one has only to see photographs of the event to feel the tragic strength and grandeur of Moiseiwitsch's designs. *Atreus* was certainly her most memorable production, a zenith in a career of pinnacles. The drawings, not as literal as those for other plays, clearly inspired all who saw them, especially the actors. The actor in the role of Electra, for example, blackened his mouth by rinsing it with vegetable dye. He told Moiseiwitsch that her drawing for Electra's mask depicted a cavernous black hole, and he dared not ruin the conception by showing the audience a fleshy pink tongue.

Many of the drawings for *Atreus* also reach artistic peaks in Moiseiwitsch's oeuvre. The pencil drawing of the Leader of the Furies (fig. no. 28) could not have been much help in the cutting room; the rapidly moving lines are only an expression of pure anger. Moiseiwitsch returned to this theme in two drawings made for the tour of the show in 1968. One, for the mask of the Eumenides (fig. no. 29, color plate 37), is executed in acrylic and India ink over white pencil on grey construction paper. Again, it could hardly have aided those in the costume shop except by raw inspiration. The face presses on the boundaries of the sheet; the edges practically explode with its power. Removed from the pressure of designing an entire production, here her talent as an artist is fully as great as her talent as a designer.

The theater is a collaborative medium; without the contributions of many the contribution of one cannot be realized. Yet, just as her gods towered over mere mortals in *The House of Atreus*, Moiseiwitsch's contribution to twentieth-century theatrical design dwarfs her fellows.

CHECKLIST

1

Set Design, Act 1
Uncle Vanya
Old Vic Theatre Company at the
New Theatre, London, 1945
Directed by John Burrell
Pencil, watercolor, pen and ink on paper,
8 x 13 1/2 (20.2 x 34.3), image
Tanya Moiseiwitsch Collection

2

Set Design for the Tilbury Scene
The Critic or a Tragedy Rehearsed
Old Vic Theatre Company at the
New Theatre, London, 1945-46
Directed by Miles Malleson
Pencil, watercolor on paper, 19 3/8 x 15
(49.3 x 38.2), image
Tanya Moiseiwitsch Collection

3

Set Design, Scene 2
Lady Rohesia
Sadler's Wells, London, 1948
Directed by Geoffrey Dunn
Watercolor, pen and brush and ink, body color
on paper, 15 3/8 x 20 3/8 (39.1 x 51.8), image
Tanya Moiseiwitsch Collection

4

Fifteen Figures, Scene 8
Henry VIII
Shakespeare Memorial Theatre,
Stratford-upon-Avon, 1949
Directed by Tyrone Guthrie
Pencil, wash, silver paint on paper,
8 1/4 x 30 (21 x 76)
Shakespeare Centre Library,
Stratford-upon-Avon

5 *

Queen Katherine, Scene 8 (Diana Wynyard)
Henry VIII
Watercolor, wash on paper,
22 x 16 (56 x 39.5)
Shakespeare Centre Library,
Stratford-upon-Avon

6*

Research Designs from Dutch Painters
The Merry Wives of Windsor
Stratford Festival Theatre, Ontario, 1956
Directed by Michael Langham
Pencil on paper, 12 1/4 x 8 1/2 (31.2 x 21.6)
Tanya Moiseiwitsch Collection

7*

Research Designs for French Breeches
The Merry Wives of Windsor
Pencil on paper, 12 1/4 x 8 1/2 (31.2 x 21.6)
Tanya Moiseiwitsch Collection

8*

Research Designs after Wenceslaus Hollar
The Merry Wives of Windsor
Pencil on paper, 12 1/4 x 8 1/2 (31.2 x 21.6)
Tanya Moiseiwitsch Collection

9

*Research Designs after Adriaen van Ostade
and Franz Hals*
The Merry Wives of Windsor
Pencil on paper, 12 1/4 x 8 1/2 (31.2 x 21.6)
Tanya Moiseiwitsch Collection

10*

*Research Designs after Gerard Terborch
and Jan Steen*
The Merry Wives of Windsor
Pencil on paper, 12 1/4 x 8 1/2 (31.2 x 21.6)
Tanya Moiseiwitsch Collection

11

Sketches of Hats
Romeo and Juliet
Stratford Festival Theatre, Ontario, 1960
Directed by Michael Langham
Pencil, ballpoint pen on paper,
13 x 8 (33 x 20.3)
The Stratford Festival, Canada

12

Studies of Birds
Volpone
Guthrie Theater, Minneapolis, 1964
Directed by Tyrone Guthrie
Pencil on paper, 10 x 7 5/16 (25.4 x 18.2)
Tanya Moiseiwitsch Collection

13

Voltore (Kenneth Ruta)
Volpone
Pencil, acrylic, brush and ink on paper,
17 3/8 x 11 (44.1 x 27.8)
Tanya Moiseiwitsch Collection

14

Cleopatra's Cloak (Zoe Caldwell)
Antony and Cleopatra
Stratford Festival Theatre, Ontario, 1967
Directed by Michael Langham
Fabric, leather, paint, beads, 78 1/2 (199.4)
The Stratford Festival, Canada

15

Cleopatra's Headdress
Antony and Cleopatra
Fabric, paint, beads, 24 (60.9)
The Stratford Festival, Canada

16

Cleopatra's Underdress
Antony and Cleopatra
Fabric, paint, beads, 73 1/4 (186)
The Stratford Festival, Canada

17
Design for Props
The Persians
Crucible Theatre, Sheffield, 1972
Directed by Colin George
Pencil, black and red felt marker on paper,
15 1/4 x 26 1/4 (38.7 x 66.8)
Tanya Moiseiwitsch Collection

18
Research Notebook
All's Well That Ends Well
Stratford Festival Theatre, Ontario, 1977
Directed by David Jones
Pencil, pen and ink on paper, 13 5/8 x 9 7/8 x
1 1/2 (34.6 x 25.1 x 3.2), closed
The Stratford Festival, Canada

19
Sir Paul Plyant (Michael Bryant)
The Double Dealer
National Theatre, London, 1978
Directed by Peter Wood
Pencil, acrylic, brush and ink, fabric swatches
on paper, 16 x 11 1/2 (40.7 x 29.2)
Tanya Moiseiwitsch Collection

20
Costume Bible
Mary Stuart
Stratford Festival Theatre, Ontario, 1982
Directed by John Hirsch
Set design by Ming Cho Lee
Color photographs, fabric swatches, marker on
paper, 16 x 11 x 2 (40.7 x 28 x 5.1), closed
The Stratford Festival, Canada

21
Set Model
Tartuffe
Stratford Festival Theatre, Ontario,
1983–84
Directed by John Hirsch
Cardboard, balsa wood, gouache, spray paint,
15 3/8 x 30 3/8 x 24 (39.1 x 77.1 x 61)
The Stratford Festival, Canada

22
Apparitions of Poverty
The Government Inspector
Stratford Festival Theatre, Ontario, 1985
Directed by Ronald Eyre
Co-designed by Polly Bohdanetsky
Papier mâché, gauze, cotton, paint, 66 (168)
The Stratford Festival, Canada

23
*Five Serfs Pulling the Mayor in His Turkish
Bath on Wheels*
The Government Inspector
Pen and ink, watercolor on paper,
8 1/4 x 11 5/8 (20.9 x 29.6)
Tanya Moiseiwitsch Collection

PLATE 1.
Set Design for the Tilbury Scene from *The Critic or a Tragedy Rehearsed*, 1945–46, cat. no. 2

PLATE 2.
Set Design, Act 1 from *Uncle Vanya*, 1945, cat. no. 1

PLATE 3.
Set Model from *Tartuffe*,
1983–84, cat. no. 21

PLATE 4.
Fifteen Figures, Scene 8 from *Henry VIII*,
1949, cat. no. 4 (photo: Shakespeare Centre
Library, Stratford-upon-Avon)

PLATE 5.
Voltore from *Volpone*,
1964, cat. no. 13

PLATE 6.
Cleopatra's Headdress from *Antony and Cleopatra*, 1967, cat. no. 15

PLATE 7.
Apparitions of Poverty from *The Government Inspector*, 1985, cat. no. 22 (photo: Carlo Catenazzi)

PLATE 8.
Kate, Act 1 from *A Summer's Day*, 1935, cat. no. 25

PLATE 9.
Neighbors: Men from *Casadh an t'Súgáin*, 1938, cat. no. 30

PLATE 10.
Neighbors: Women from *Casadh an t'Súgáin*, 1938, cat. no. 31

PLATE 11.
Set Design, Act 4 from
Cyrano de Bergerac, 1946,
cat. no. 34

PLATE 12.
Cyrano de Bergerac from *Cyrano de Bergerac*, 1946, cat. no. 37

PLATE 13.
*De Guiche, Act 1 from Cyrano
de Bergerac*, 1946, cat. no. 40

PLATE 14.
Montfleury from *Cyrano de
Bergerac*, 1946, cat. no. 41

PLATE 15.
Design for Interlude Cloth from
Peter Grimes, 1947, cat. no. 45
(photo: Collections of the Theatre
Museum. By courtesy of the
Board of Trustees of the Victoria
and Albert Museum, London)

PLATE 16.
Set Design for Grimes's Hut
from *Peter Grimes*, 1947,
cat. no. 44

PLATE 17.
Ned Keene from *Peter Grimes*,
1947, cat. no. 49

Peter Grimes
NIECE II
Act III

TO BE DYED,

PLATE 18.
Niece II, Act 3 from *Peter Grimes,*
1947, cat. no. 50

PLATE 20.
Inn Types and Citizens: The Sheriff and Men, Scenes 7 and 10 from *Henry IV, Part I*, 1951, cat. no. 59 (photo: Shakespeare Centre Library, Stratford-upon-Avon)

PLATE 19.
Acolyte, Scene 14 from *Henry IV, Part I*, 1951, cat. no. 56 (photo: Shakespeare Centre Library, Stratford-upon-Avon)

PLATE 21.
Inn Types and Citizens: Women from *Henry IV, Part I*, 1951, cat. no. 60 (photo: Shakespeare Centre Library, Stratford-upon-Avon)

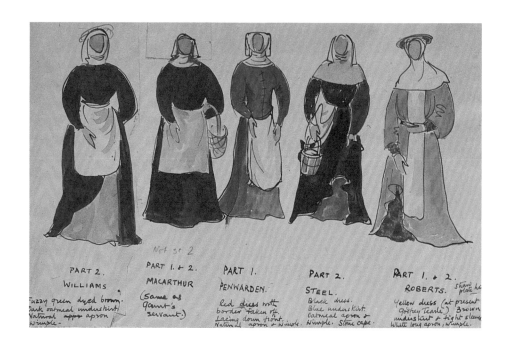

Fang and Snare
Abruza & Henchie.

Henry IV
part 2.

PLATE 22.
Fang and Snare from *Henry IV, Part II*, 1951, cat. no. 61
(photo: Shakespeare Centre Library, Stratford-upon-Avon)

PLATE 23.
Rumour after Casting Cloak Away
from *Henry IV, Part II*, 1951, cat.
no. 63 (photo: Shakespeare Centre
Library, Stratford-upon-Avon)

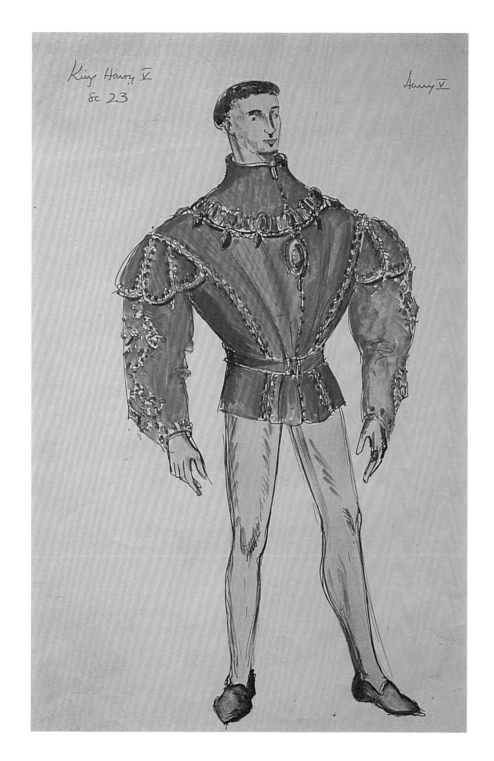

PLATE 24.
King Henry V, Scene 23 from
Henry V, 1951, cat. no. 64
(photo: Shakespeare Centre
Library, Stratford-upon-Avon)

Mr Alec Guinness.
⑧

Richard III
Sc 15 Coronation
Over.robe to cou
the

PLATE 25.
King Richard III, Scene 15 from *Richard III*, 1953, cat. no. 71

PLATE 26.
Lord Mayor, Scenes 7, 11, and 13 from *Richard III*, 1953,
cat. no. 73

PLATE 27.
Queen Margaret from *Richard III*, 1953, cat. no. 74

PLATE 28.
Autolicus from *The Winter's Tale*,
1958, cat. no. 79

PLATE 29.
Camillo, A Lord of Sicilia, Act 1
from *The Winter's Tale*, 1958,
cat. no. 80

Hermione

3

The Winter's Tale.

TM.
1958

PLATE 30.
Hermione, Act 3 from *The Winter's Tale*, 1958, cat. no. 83

PLATE 31.
Agamemnon from *The House of Atreus*, 1967,
cat. no. 100

PLATE 32.
Mask of Agamemnon from
The House of Atreus, 1967,
cat. no. 108

PLATE 33.
Head of Pallas Athena from
The House of Atreus, 1967,
cat. no. 110

PLATE 34.
Helmet from *The House of
Atreus*, 1967, cat. no. 114

PLATE 35.
Athena from *The House of Atreus*, 1967, cat. no. 101

PLATE 36.
Clytemnestra from *The House of Atreus*, 1967, cat. no. 103

PLATE 37.
Mask Design for the Eumenides
from *The House of Atreus*, 1967,
cat. no. 104

PLATE 38.
Corpse's Head (Clytemnestra) from *The House
of Atreus*, 1967, cat. no. 113

PLATE 39.
Robert Pastene as Aegisthus and Douglas Campbell as Clytemnestra present
Agamemnon's body to the Furies in *The House of Atreus*, Guthrie Theater,
Minneapolis, 1967 (photo: Don Getsug Studios)

PLATE 40.
Set Design from *Phaedra Britannica*, 1975,
cat. no. 117

PLATE 41.
Set Model from *Phaedra Britannica*, 1975,
cat. no. 118

PLATE 42.
Burleigh from *Phaedra Britannica*,
1975, cat. no. 121

PLATE 43.
Lilamani from *Phaedra Britannica*, 1975,
cat. no. 123

PLATE 44.
The Memsahib from *Phaedra Britannica*, 1975, cat. no. 124

DENNIS BEHL

A Career in the Theater

Youthful Beginnings

IT WAS THE SUMMER of 1935. Tanya Moiseiwitsch, aged twenty-one, was on an English ship bound for Dublin, embarking on a life in the theater as a designer. Looking forward to three months of work at Ireland's celebrated Abbey Theatre, she could not know that this brief engagement would actually last three years and launch a vocation of more than half a century. On the brink of her future, crossing the Irish Sea, the young woman began to ponder. Whom would she miss most? Her parents? Her stepfather, who had nurtured her theatrical interests? Her teachers and the familiar atmosphere of London's Central School of Arts and Crafts? Or the backstage community at the Old Vic, where she had served the past six months as an apprentice?

Born into a world of music, Moiseiwitsch, daughter of concert violinist Daisy Kennedy and pianist Benno Moiseiwitsch, was accustomed to international travel. Her earliest memories were of packing off by ship or train, moving on to the next city, the next hotel. Her father, during his fifty-two-year career, toured the South Pacific, Asia, South America, and South Africa, holding audiences spellbound with his dazzling technique. Kennedy, a scholar of Elder Conservatorium in Adelaide, South Australia, and a pupil of Otakar Sevcik in Prague, had made her debut in Vienna, and first performed in London in 1911. She toured Europe and America, and joined her husband in recitals during his Australian tour of 1919. Their daughter learned to play the Irish harp and piano, and practiced daily even while the family traveled.

"The concert tours were the most grueling, exhausting, and nerve-wracking existences for both my parents," Moiseiwitsch recalls. "I was very much aware of continuous practicing at home…in hotels…in trains…on dummy piano keyboards… on ship. And practicing is what I remember with much more pleasure than the public performances." Despite the public character of her parents' life, Moiseiwitsch says that as a child, she was influenced not to be a public person. "Even as an adult," she says, "my great fear is people getting up in public and making mistakes or letting down their very, very high standard."[1] After all, her father had won the Anton Rubenstein Prize at the Imperial School of Music in his native Odessa at the age of nine, and her mother had learned to read music at four and won a music scholarship by the age of thirteen. What would be expected of the progeny of such a union?

Moiseiwitsch was not destined to become a musician, for no matter how diligently she practiced, she could not excel at the piano. When her father would return from a tour abroad, she was urged to learn a piece and play it for him. She still remembers the agony: "The performance was so poor, however hard you worked…. You were thanked and praised and told, 'we'll try again.' It was so obvious that I wasn't going to make the grade. I saw the handwriting on the wall before anyone pointed it out to me."[2] She came to understand that she wanted to succeed on her own terms, in her own way, and she abandoned plans for a career in music. Enrolled in private English schools, Moiseiwitsch proved particular about what she would learn, applying herself only to subjects she enjoyed. History, poetry, painting, and drawing were her favorites, and all of these, she later realized, connected in various ways with the theater.

In 1924, Moiseiwitsch's parents divorced. Kennedy married the playwright John Drinkwater, and soon after, Tanya and her sister, Sandra, moved to Brampton, Huntingdonshire, to live with their mother and stepfather. Drinkwater had a broad theatrical understanding, and it was through him that Moiseiwitsch was to develop a serious interest in theater. She often accompanied Drinkwater and her mother to performances, especially at the Old Vic, and she met his circle of literary friends, which included James Joyce and George Bernard Shaw. "I benefited from a wonderful upbringing with my mother's second husband," Moiseiwitsch would later recall. "His life in the theater was very glamorous—he wrote plays, acted in them, directed them, and also wrote poetry. So I got interested in that side of life, which perhaps, I might not have otherwise."[3]

Moiseiwitsch had actually been introduced to the theater at a very young age when she was taken to see a matinee of *The Blue Bird*. That night, she came to dinner with a tablecloth over her head and informed her parents, "I am light." For a while she thought she might like to become an actress.[4] In school plays, however, she must have overacted, because she remembers being asked to "pipe down a bit." Her terror of performing ultimately short-circuited her ambition to tread the boards. By the time she was a teenager, it was becoming clear that for her, work in the theater was not *on* stage. Backstage work, on the other hand, with its sense of community effort, appealed strongly to Moiseiwitsch. Her stepfather advised that backstage she could be useful without being seen, and have no need to be frightened.

In 1930, Moiseiwitsch enrolled in the Central School of Arts and Crafts, an important decision considering the history of the

institution, its philosophy, faculty, and methods of instruction. Known today as Central/St. Martins, the school had been established in 1896 by William R. Lethaby (1857–1931), a disciple of William Morris, the great Victorian artist-designer and founder of the Arts and Crafts movement in England. Morris believed that everyone ought to be taught to draw, just as everyone ought to be taught to read and write. He advocated that artist and designer should be "practically one," and that the "designer should learn the practical way of carrying out the work for which he designs."[5] These theories were perpetuated by the Central School, which, until the Bauhaus, was considered the most progressive art school in Europe.[6]

The school prospectus at the time Moiseiwitsch was admitted declared its fundamental aim and method in the teaching of arts and crafts was production. There were facilities for silversmithing, furniture making, textiles, painted and sculpted architectural decoration, stained glass, book production, engraving, and lithography. Although there were no courses in theater design as such, and no courses in scenic design until 1937,[7] the textile department offered a class in heraldry for theatrical purposes, and the costume department provided instruction in historical costumes, dress design, and, according to the prospectus, "treatment of material for stage purposes and fashion drawing." The costume offerings attracted Moiseiwitsch's interest the most.

Following Morris's philosophy, Central School's instructors were practicing designers, assisted by part-time teachers, "so that the designers could, without abandoning their profession, convey something of its practical realities to their students."[8] The head of the costume school, for example, carried on her profession of costumier from her Bedford Square shop. Jeannetta Cochrane was engaged professionally by the West End theaters and had designed *Hamlet* and *Love for Love* for John Gielgud. Later, she advised the prestigious Heal's Furniture Company, whose clients included the royal family. Cochrane taught that the historical costume should be patterned according to the cut of the clothing of the epoch. To determine the appropriate cut, the artist must research paintings and prints to find evidence contemporary to the period. Thus, Cochrane's students took five-hour weekly visits to the Victoria and Albert Museum to study the collection and to hear lectures by noted costume historian James Laver and art and architectural historian Bannister Fletcher.

The impact of Cochrane's instruction can be seen in the work of her students, who included, besides Moiseiwitsch, Alix Stone, David Walker, and the author of *Corsets and Crinolines* and *The Cut of Men's Clothes 1600–1900*, Nora Waugh. Stone recalls that, in addition to historical research, Cochrane taught by example that design should be used intelligently, not superficially, and that the execution of the costume should always be a well-crafted job.[9] Moiseiwitsch, who adopted this high standard of craftsmanship, remembers Cochrane's insistence on the student's ability to observe and self-initiate: "She never told you anything you wanted to know. She was absolutely brilliant in keeping you interested, by telling you all the things that had happened to her in the theater … but when you wanted to know how to cut a leg-o'-mutton sleeve, one of her assistants would say in a voice of doom, 'I can't *teach* you anything, but you can *learn* if you like.'"[10] The emphasis was on self-reliance and resourcefulness.

During the 1931–32 season, while one of Drinkwater's plays was being performed at the Old Vic, Moiseiwitsch met Lilian Baylis, the legendary manager of the company. The costume department needed help in making hats, so Moiseiwitsch volunteered her services. Each year, two students trained with the Old Vic's staff scenic artist, Leslie Young, as interns on the paint frame. Would-be apprentices competed in a drawing contest judged by Baylis, who charged the winners a fee to work at her theater. Thus, after completing only two of her three years at Central School, Moiseiwitsch found herself working at the Old Vic "mixing paint for a stream of designers of ballet, Shakespeare, and opera."[11] Because the Old Vic staff also managed the Sadler's Wells Theatre and its ballet company, the scenic painting assignments ran the gamut from modern ballet to elaborate period settings.

Productions alternated between theaters, and many of Moiseiwitsch's apprentice days were spent traveling between the two houses, laden with heavy paint buckets. While slapping size on canvas flats, painting props, cleaning paint pots, or figuring how to enlarge a design from scaled drawings, she was, in fact, learning the technical skills of mounting and running a show. Baylis worked her in almost every department, not just on the paint frame. The labor was demanding, and necessary: "You can make apprentices work so hard," Moiseiwitsch noted, "and for such hours that they get put off the theater altogether, [but] on the other hand if they are going to get any place then it's salutary because they know how hard the job is, that it isn't sitting in a studio thinking up lovely colors."[12]

Moiseiwitsch valued most the opportunities to watch procedures without yet having the responsibility for making decisions or resolving crises. She discovered that problems were most often solved with basic leadership qualities, by delegating authority and using common sense. Her apprenticeship also brought her into contact with "brilliant young people who had a sense of purpose, like Charles Laughton, Flora Robson, and Tyrone Guthrie [who] was the director, and the different designers for each play, opera, and ballet," she recalled. "So I had plenty of incentive and it was stimulating to work in such a vigorous atmosphere."[13]

Following her apprenticeship, Moiseiwitsch was hired as an assistant to designer Ruth Keating at the Westminster Theatre, where Hugh Hunt directed the weekly repertory of classical and modern plays, including comedies and thrillers. Keating taught her assistant to be as efficient as possible in achieving the best effect on stage. But the Westminster experience presented unexpected demands; Moiseiwitsch was startled to find that her task was to make shoes. "I knew nothing about making shoes," she said, "but I soon found out, because if the actors came in to try them on, and they weren't ready, your face was red."[14] This regard for actors' needs became characteristic of her attitude. "Tanya was much more patient with actors than I," said Keating, recalling that 1934-35 season.[15] When the Royal Academy of Dramatic Arts presented two student productions, *The Faithful* and *Alien Corn*, on the Westminster stage, Moiseiwitsch, herself still a student, got her first design job. The scenery was her weakness; even her scale-model settings tended to topple, she confessed. Fortunately, the director knew exactly what he wanted. "I must have managed to do what I was told, because in the end I went off with £5 in my pocket," laughed the designer.[16]

Hunt was favorably impressed with this young and highly promising talent and asked Moiseiwitsch to accompany him as the designer for the summer of 1935 at the Abbey Theatre. Although the thought of becoming a full-fledged designer at this point was frightening, her lack of experience was actually an advantage. In retrospect, Moiseiwitsch realized that Hunt "really wanted to do the designing himself, but he wanted someone to carry out his work for him.... This was ideal for me because I was so inexperienced, I would *have* to be told what to do."[17] The Abbey summer season turned into a three-year run for which Moiseiwitsch created settings and costumes for nearly fifty productions. The weekly repertory system forced her into quick decisions and required efficient use of time and material. After three years, Moiseiwitsch could proudly say, "I was doing a great deal on my own, but never totally alone, because I very strongly believe that a designer works with the director and that he tells you far more than you ever tell him."[18]

NOTES

1. Tanya Moiseiwitsch, interview by Moyelyn Merchant, 8 April 1975, Canadian Broadcasting Company Radio Archives, Toronto.

2. Ibid.

3. Moiseiwitsch, interview with the author, Stratford, Ontario, 24 June 1992. John Drinkwater's success as a playwright was firmly established with *Abraham Lincoln* (1918), *Oliver Cromwell* (1921), *Mary Stuart* (1922), *Robert E. Lee* (1923), and *Bird in Hand* (1927). He often opened his works at the Birmingham Repertory Theatre, where he produced over sixty plays, then transferred them to London.

4. Moiseiwitsch, interview by Robert T. Smith, *Minneapolis Star*, 17 March 1976.

5. "Around the Art School: The L.C.C. Central School of Arts and Crafts," *The Artist* 43 (April 1952): 38–40.

6. See Gillian Naylor, *The Arts and Crafts Movement: A Study of Its Sources, Ideals and Influence on Design Theory* (Cambridge, Mass.: M.I.T. Press, 1971), 179.

7. Ruth Keating, an instructor at the Central School, writes that until she "started a class in set design there in about 1937, this was not taught at Central." (Letter from Keating to the author, 3 December 1979.) The point is that Moiseiwitsch was not trained as a designer of stage sets at the Central School, though architecture was covered in some courses offered at the time she attended.

8. Naylor, *Arts and Crafts Movement*, 179.

9. Alix Stone, interview with the author, Lyric Opera House, Hammersmith, England, 10 December 1979.

10. Moiseiwitsch, "The Director and the Designer," International Lecture Series panel discussion with Herbert Whittaker and Murry Lauffer, Ontario College of Art, 24 May 1979. Stratford Festival Archives, Stratford, Ontario.

11. Moiseiwitsch, interviewed by Peter Jackson, "Pioneer in Design," *Plays and Players* 8 (February 1960): 6. Hereafter cited as "Jackson interview."

12. Moiseiwitsch, "The Director and the Designer."

13. Jackson interview, 6.

14. Moiseiwitsch, quoted in Roy Newquist, *Showcase* (New York: William Morrow & Company, 1966), 277–78. Hereafter cited as "Newquist interview."

15. Keating, personal letter to author, 3 December 1979.

16. Moiseiwitsch, interview with the author, London, 24 March 1993.

17. Newquist interview.

18. Jackson interview, 6.

The Abbey Theatre Years

1935–1938

IT IS AN AUSPICIOUS place to start a career, the Abbey Theatre. Opening its doors on 27 December 1904, the Abbey had merged the literary talents of the Irish Literary Theatre's William Butler Yeats, Lady Augusta Gregory, and Edward Martyn with the acting experience of the Fay brothers' Irish National Theatre Society to lay the foundations for one of the most influential cultural institutions in the world. In 1924, the Abbey had the distinction of becoming the first government-subsidized theater in an English-speaking nation, when the Irish Free State began awarding an annual grant for the playhouse's operation. The Abbey was to become inextricably linked with Ireland's dramatic heritage, and to this day continues as a leader in world drama. By the 1930s, the playhouse had a history rich with the literary fire of its founders and of St. John Ervine, Sean O'Casey, Lennox Robinson, George Bernard Shaw, and J. M. Synge. This extraordinary dramatic tradition was illuminated by the brilliant acting of Sara Allgood, Dudley Diggs, Frank and Willie Fay, Barry Fitzgerald, F. J. McCormick, Maire O'Neill, and Arthur Sinclair, to name but a few company members. When Tanya Moiseiwitsch arrived with director Hugh Hunt in 1935, the Abbey had completed numerous international tours, including six to America, and would complete a seventh during her tenure there as designer.

Moiseiwitsch would emerge as the Abbey's first resident designer, if not in name, then most certainly in practice. But while the Abbey was an auspicious venue, it also might be thought an unlikely place for a couple of English transplants to take root. Artistically, this was the home of the Irish peasant play and the beacon of the Gaelic language movement. The Abbey style was anchored in ideas expounded in 1906 by Yeats who, with his literary colleagues, stated that Abbey writers "have taken their types and scenes direct from Irish life,...rich in dramatic materials... exuberant language...primitive grace and wildness...[and] a

vividness and color unknown in more civilized places." Both the author's and acting company's desire, he continued, was to "put upon the stage the actual life and aims of the peasants they have so carefully studied in their native land."[1]

What did this mean for the visual elements of scenery and stage properties? Interiors employed "unique fac-similes [sic] of originals...[and] the properties were all taken directly from the cottages of peasantry."[2] A real spinning wheel, for instance, had been in use near Gort for over a hundred years until it was bought by Lady Gregory as a prop for the Abbey stage. An aesthetic style—some call realism—had a firm grasp, perhaps a stranglehold, at the Abbey for nearly thirty years. "From 1914 onwards," observed Hunt, "the dreary repetition of white-washed cottage kitchen and wall-papered parlor has been only occasionally relieved by an imaginative design."[3] Ironically, the fresh scenic innovations sought by the founders of the Irish dramatic renaissance at the turn of the century had become time-honored, cherished in their own right, and finally, stultifying conventions chafing upon the creative energy of another generation.

Nevertheless, conditions at this particular moment in 1935 were, if not nurturing for a young English designer, at least fertile. The Abbey's board was simultaneously impressed and alarmed by the rising success of their rival Dublin company, the Gate Theatre, founded in 1928 by English actor Hilton Edwards and Irish director Michael MacLiammoir. With the manipulation and urging of Yeats, the Abbey's board decided to compete by also producing foreign plays, thus fundamentally broadening its original mission to produce only plays by Irish authors or about Irish subjects. Seeking to sharpen the competition, the board assigned Hunt and Moiseiwitsch to the non-Irish productions ushered in by the Abbey's new policy. In Hunt, the Abbey leadership recognized a director with a proven track record with classical and foreign masterpieces at Croydon Repertory Theatre and London's Westminster Theatre. In Moiseiwitsch, Hunt recognized a willing and promising young artist who was open to suggestion.

She accepted that "he wanted to have a big hand in the design of the sets, because he knew exactly what he wanted." As for the costumes, "he would not say a thing," Moiseiwitsch recalled. If she seemed tentative for lack of experience, she was also on the edge of epiphany. She would discover that "finding out what the director has in mind," is an invaluable skill for a designer.[4] This attitude became a working principle for Moiseiwitsch not only during these formative years but throughout her career. At this early period in her development, she understandably depended on Hunt to guide her, and over the years she continued to find that preliminary discussions of the text and the director's plans for staging it affected every aspect of her design. Her three-month trial as Hunt's designer, though enormously intense, proved to be intensely rewarding.

The challenge before her now was daunting by any measure, since the playhouse presented a show a week and the curtain seemed always to be going up. Two previous offerings would be revived from the company's repertory, polished up with only one rehearsal, and every third week a totally new work was born. The Abbey's tight time and budget restraints afforded no delays due to miscommunication. Moiseiwitsch's first assignment was a new work by F. R. Higgins, a poet and friend of Yeats, who served on the Abbey board of directors. Leading actor Michael J. Dolan directed and played in *A Deuce o' Jacks*. Opening night was slated for 16 September, only a few weeks after Moiseiwitsch's August arrival. It was not a critical success. "It was the only play ever performed at the Abbey which the audience forgot to applaud," wrote Abbey scholar Peter Kavanagh. "*A Deuce o' Jacks* lacked every quality essential to a play. It had not form, nor plot, nor poetry."[5]

But the play *did* have a setting and costumes, considered by avid first-nighter and diarist Joseph Holloway to be "too fantastical for words." Holloway reported how "the piece opened in the dark. In order to get up a wake, 'Luke Gaffney' who was the dead spirit of 'Zozimus' arrives on the scene, and the entry of a priest stops all the mad, noisy dancing and singing. In the midst of the

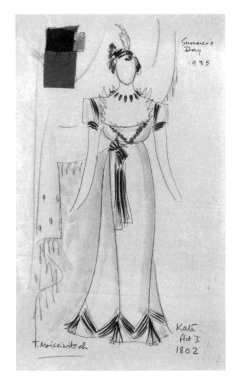

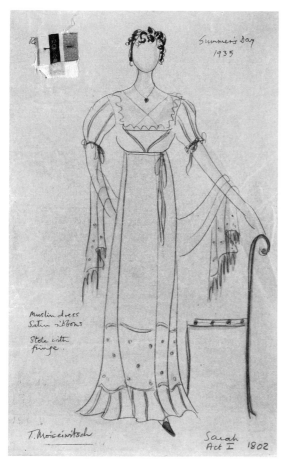

32

30. *Amelia, Acts 2 and 3* from *A Summer's Day*, 1935, cat. no. 24

31. *Kate, Act 1* from *A Summer's Day*, 1935, cat. no. 25

32. *Sarah, Act 1* from *A Summer's Day*, 1935, cat. no. 26

crowd of hawkers, all tattered and torn...'Pharaoh's daughter' and 'Jezebel' dance a ballet attired in scanty attire. One felt, while the piece was in progress, that a few more such performances and the traditions of the Abbey would be no more."[6]

Just fourteen days after the ill-fated hand of *A Deuce o' Jacks* had been dealt, Moiseiwitsch faced the opening of *A Village Wooing*, a modest work by Shaw. Her opening nautical scene placed the ships' masts and funnels at odd angles. Pennants and life belts were emblazoned with the author's initials, "GBS." While it may have "belonged to the cockeyed school of art," wrote the *New York Times* drama critic, "somehow this fantastic setting matched the mood of the play."[7] The opinionated Holloway recorded that "the designs for settings went to prove that all modern scenery was always seen through the eyes of an intoxicated man. All out of plumb and toppling over."[8] This effect was particularly disconcerting to Holloway—who was the architect of the Abbey's fine stone building.

Also in 1935, *The Well of the Saints*, Synge's first attempt at the full three-act dramatic form (1905), was brought back to the Abbey stage in a new production designed by Moiseiwitsch. Set in "some lonely mountainous district in the east of Ireland one or more centuries ago," the story concerns Martin and Mary Doul, blind beggars, who have been kindly deceived by townsfolk into believing they are beautiful. When their sight is temporarily restored by water from a miraculous well, harsh reality causes the couple to part. But the cure is temporary, and as darkness descends, reunited Mary and Martin refuse permanent sight, preferring the dream of perfection. Moiseiwitsch's design for the second act reinforced, in its elemental simplicity, Synge's poetic metaphor of fire and water. Set along the village roadside, cluttered with broken wheels, a fiery forge glowed at one side of the stage. Martin sat nearby in the shadows, cutting sticks, and a stone well covered with a board stood near the center of the scene.

By December, Moiseiwitsch's presence was beginning to be felt and appreciated. The same *New York Times* critic remarked that with productions like André Obey's *Noah*, which she designed, "the Abbey is shaking itself free from the slavish peasant drama tradition that had already begun to threaten its existence, and for this drama lovers in Dublin are thankful."[9] Behind the scenes, the Hunt-Moiseiwitsch team had been given a nod of approval as well: Hunt was appointed manager. By spring of 1936, the policy of presenting non-Irish plays was abandoned. Shaw's *Candida* and *Village Wooing*, Obey's *Noah* and *Coriolanus*, and James Elroy Flecker's *Hassan* "neither recaptured the so-called 'lively minds' who had deserted to the Gate, nor pleased the groundlings of the Abbey," observed Hunt. "Clearly, the Irish theater could not be rescued by challenging the Gate's policy." He concluded that the Abbey's "immediate regeneration lay in a vigorous and creative approach to the work upon which its national and international reputation had been founded."[10]

The theater had produced only two new one-act plays in 1935. In 1936, the Abbey produced nine full-length plays and ten the following year, with three new one-acters. The increased activity, according to Frank O'Connor, "was largely due to Hunt who, eager for work, read every possible play."[11] With this infusion of energy, Moiseiwitsch was responsible for the design of a full range of drama: new plays, classic non-Irish works, and revivals of earlier Abbey productions. Now in control, Hunt was adamant in his conviction that "the standards of visual presentation had to be improved if the theater was to keep abreast of the new movements in scenography, and the same care [must be] given to the design of farm kitchen and Dublin tenement as was given in the past to the plays of Yeats and Gregory." One can only imagine to what degree standards had previously slipped when one reads, "Players must no longer be required to rummage in the wardrobe to find suitable costumes for themselves, nor must the peasant girls in *The Playboy* [*of the Western World*] adorn themselves with eyeshadow and permanently waved hair."[12]

Moiseiwitsch was about to learn that revitalizing these native works, many encrusted with tradition, could prove a dicey business. Reviving Synge's 1905 classic *The Playboy of the Western World* in 1936, Hunt insisted that younger players must take the place of those who had outgrown their parts. His discussions with Moiseiwitsch led to modifying the original ground plan by "moving a door or window six inches." The result? "I nearly got massacred by the company," Moiseiwitsch remembers, "'Who does she think she is?'"[13] Higgins clashed with Hunt over the look, accent, and direction of the production, which was not a carbon copy of the original. According to Hunt, it was Moiseiwitsch's tact and the senior players' support that enabled him to effect the desired changes without causing open hostility among players and staff.[14] Reacting to this new design for *The Playboy*, Holloway wrote that "the new setting proved effective."[15] *Irish Times* critic A. E. Malone pointed out, "This revival will not hearten the traditionalists of the Abbey...but it is surely time another mode has its day."[16]

As time passed, Moiseiwitsch gained confidence and proved that she had come into her own. The 1937 revival of Robinson's *The Lost Leader* (1918) is a case in point. The play proposed that Charles Stewart Parnell, whom many considered Ireland's greatest leader, had not died; suffering from amnesia, he worked as a porter in a small hotel in western Ireland. The action begins with a hypnotist unraveling the old man's secret. Parnell appeals for fellowship in a strife-torn nation, but is lost again, accidently killed by a rock hurled by a blind man. Moiseiwitsch's scenery, particularly for act 3, was a masterpiece of pictorial illusion. The lights came up slowly to reveal the huge standing stones of Croaghpatrick, dwarfing the surrounding slopes. In the distance, larger hills were barely visible, as the sun had set in the western sky. One character sat smoking in silence. Moiseiwitsch "made a beautiful production of it," recalled a member of the audience, "and the opening of the third act is the only occasion...of a decor [at the Abbey] being applauded in its own right."[16]

Douglas Hyde's *Casadh an t'Súgáin* (*Twisting of the Rope*) (fig. nos. 33–36, color plates 9, 10) must have given Hunt and Moiseiwitsch some trepidation as they prepared for its return to the stage in 1938. The author was renowned as a scholar, poet,

33. *Neighbors: Men* from *Casadh an t'Súgáin*, 1938, cat. no. 30

34. *Neighbors: Women* from *Casadh an t'Súgáin*, 1938, cat. no. 31

35. *Shela and Maire* from *Casadh an t'Súgáin*, 1938, cat. no. 32

36. *Tumas and Una* from *Casadh an t'Súgáin*, 1938, cat. no. 33

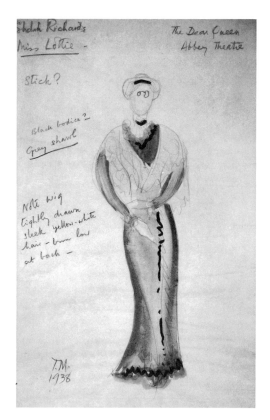

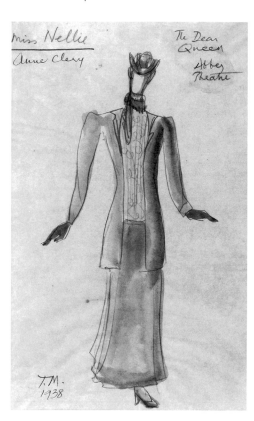

37. *Miss Lottie* from *The Dear Queen*, 1938, cat. no. 27

38. *Miss Nellie* from *The Dear Queen*, 1938, cat. no. 28

39. *Miss Sophie* from *The Dear Queen*, 1938, cat. no. 29

translator, and founder of the Gaelic League—and had just been appointed the first President of the Republic of Ireland. His one-act play, considered to be the first Gaelic text produced in any theater, had been premiered in 1901 by the Irish Literary Theatre. The plot concerns a youth who has his heart set on the girl of a house where he is a caller. To get rid of him, the family schemes for a new hay rope to be twisted. The young man, proud of his ability as a rope-twister, sets about his task with his back to an open door. Bragging, flirting, twisting, he moves backward until he finally falls through the doorway. With the door slammed upon him, his shouts filling the air, the curtain falls. "Slight as it was," wrote Synge in 1906, this play "gave new direction and impulse to Irish drama."[18] The Hunt-Moiseiwitsch restaging was "brightly

and fantastically set, and," according to Holloway, "the costumes were a little on the idealistic side."[19] Moiseiwitsch's bright sketches show the trammels of realism had been released.

The Abbey's renewed spirit and ambition stimulated others to develop their talents. A dentist, Andrew Ganly, was inspired to try his hand at a play, which premiered 4 April 1938. In *The Dear Queen*, Ganly spun a tale of three sisters of Blake Hall, who tragically cut themselves off from the present and cling to a Victorian past—until a Reverend Mum brings dramatic changes to their lives. Moiseiwitsch's settings and costumes for *The Dear Queen* were "striking and appropriate," according to the *Dublin Evening Mail*'s reviewer. Her renderings for the costumes (fig. nos. 37–39) are quick watercolor washes, prepared under the pressure of a busy wardrobe schedule, with a warm iron applied to speed their drying time. Simple, direct, and colorful, they communicated the period and mood, "just as I imagined they would look," said the *Evening Mail*'s new writer.[20]

After Hunt's departure from the Abbey Theatre in November 1938, Moiseiwitsch soon followed his example, leaving Dublin to seek new challenges. But her influence at the Abbey continued to be felt. Her successor in coming seasons was Yeats's daughter Anne, who had assisted Moiseiwitsch in the Abbey's scenery and costume department. With the practical experience gained under Moiseiwitsch's tutelage, Anne Yeats would design seventeen productions over the next eleven years. Hunt went on to distinguish himself, serving as director of the Bristol Old Vic (1945), the Old Vic in London (1948), and the Elizabethan Theatre Trust in Australia (1955). He became the first professor of drama at Manchester University, and was again appointed artistic director of the Abbey Theatre in 1969.

Nearly two decades after introducing his young designer to the Abbey, Hunt addressed his class at Manchester University about play production, teaching the same lesson he must have shared with Moiseiwitsch: "The theater, like all the arts, is more easily analyzed by practice, than by theory.... For all its mystique, its emotions, its ephemeral existence, the play on stage is nine-tenths a matter of craftsmanship, planning, and clear thinking." Moiseiwitsch returned to the Abbey to collaborate with Hunt on O'Casey's *Red Roses for Me* in 1980, revisiting a working relationship established so many years earlier: "How much or how little the director suggests to the designer," Hunt wrote, "must depend on the qualities and abilities of each of them.... They must endeavor to work as one mind, contributing to a single vision."[21]

NOTES

1. William Butler Yeats et al., "Illustrated Programme Distributed in Cardiff, Glasgow, Aberdeen, Newcastle, Edinburgh, Hull, 26 May to 9 July 1906," in *The Abbey Theatre: Interviews and Recollections*, edited by E. H. Mikhail (Totowa, N.J.: Barnes and Noble, 1988), 317–18.

2. Ibid.

3. Hugh Hunt, *The Abbey: Ireland's National Theatre, 1904–1979* (New York: Columbia University Press, 1979), 153.

4. Moiseiwitsch, interview with the author, London, 24 March 1993, hereafter cited as "author interview."

5. Peter Kavanagh, *The Story of The Abbey Theatre* (New York: The Devin-Adair Company, 1950), 171.

6. Joseph Holloway, *Joseph Holloway's Irish Theatre*, vol. 2, edited by Robert Hogan and Michael J. O'Neill (Dixon, Calif.: Proscenium Press, 1968), 48.

7. Hugh Smith, *New York Times*, 27 October 1935.

8. Holloway, *Holloway's Irish Theatre*, 2:49.

9. Smith, *New York Times*, 1 December 1935.

10. Hunt, *The Abbey*, 153.

11. Frank O'Connor, "Myself and the Abbey Theatre," in *Interviews and Recollections*, 151.

12. Hunt, *The Abbey*, 154.

13. Moiseiwitsch, author interview.

14. Hunt, *The Abbey*, 154.

15. Holloway, *Holloway's Irish Theatre*, 2:56.

16. A. E. Malone, quoted in Hunt, *The Abbey*, 154.

17. Frank O'Connor, *My Father's Son* (New York: Alfred A. Knopf, 1969), 192.

18. J. M. Synge, "The Dramatic Movement in Ireland," in *Interviews and Recollections*, 54.

19. Holloway, *Holloway's Irish Theatre*, 3:9.

20. *Dublin Evening Mail*, April 1938.

21. Hunt, *The Director in the Theatre* (London: Routledge and Kegan Paul, 1954), 4 and 56.

ABBEY THEATRE

24
Amelia, Acts 2 and 3 (May Craig)
A Summer's Day
Abbey Theatre, Dublin, 1935
Directed by Hugh Hunt
Pencil, watercolor, fabric swatches on paper,
14 7/8 x 9 1/2 (37.8 x 24.2)
The Stratford Festival, Canada

25
Kate, Act 1 (Ria Mooney)
A Summer's Day
Pencil, watercolor, pen and ink, fabric swatches
on paper, 14 7/8 x 9 1/2 (37.8 x 24.2)
The Stratford Festival, Canada

26
Sarah, Act 1 (Moya Devlin)
A Summer's Day
Pencil, watercolor, fabric swatches on paper,
14 1/2 x 9 3/8 (36.8 x 23.8)
The Stratford Festival, Canada

27
Miss Lottie (Shelah Richards)
The Dear Queen
Abbey Theatre, Dublin, 1938
Directed by Hugh Hunt
Pencil, watercolor, brush and ink on paper,
15 x 9 3/4 (38 x 24.8)
The Stratford Festival, Canada

28
Miss Nellie (Ann Clery)
The Dear Queen
Pencil, watercolor on paper,
14 7/8 x 10 1/2 (37.8 x 25.7)
The Stratford Festival, Canada

29
Miss Sophie (Christine Hayden)
The Dear Queen
Pencil, watercolor on paper,
14 7/8 x 10 1/8 (37.8 x 25.7)
The Stratford Festival, Canada

30
Neighbors: Men (W. O'Gorman, John
McDarby, O'Rourke, M. Kinsella)
Casadh an t'Súgaín (Twisting of the Rope)
Abbey Theatre, Dublin, 1938
Directed by Hugh Hunt
Pencil, watercolor on paper mounted on mat
with crayon notations, 9 5/8 x 14 (24.5 x
35.5), sheet; 11 3/4 x 15 1/2 (29.8 x 39.8), mat
The Stratford Festival, Canada

31
Neighbors: Women (Florence Lynch, Moya
Devlin, Phyllis Ryan, Shelah Ward)
Casadh an t'Súgaín (Twisting of the Rope)
Pencil, watercolor on paper mounted on mat
with crayon notations, 9 3/4 x 14
(24.8 x 35.5), sheet; 11 3/4 x 16 1/8
(29.8 x 41.3), mat
The Stratford Festival, Canada

32
Shela and Maire (Nora O'Mahoney and
Josephine Fitzgerald)
Casadh an t'Súgaín (Twisting of the Rope)
Pencil, watercolor on paper mounted on mat
with crayon notations, 9 1/8 x 6 3/8
(23.2 x 16.2), sheet (*Shela*); 9 1/4 x 6 1/4
(23.5 x 15.5), sheet (*Maire*); 11 3/4 x 15 1/2
(29.8 x 39.8), mat
The Stratford Festival, Canada

33
Tumas and Una (Cyril Cusack and Brid ni
Loinsigh)
Casadh an t'Súgaín (Twisting of the Rope)
Pencil, watercolor on paper mounted on mat
with crayon notations, 9 x 6 3/8 (22.8 x 16.2),
sheet (*Tumas*); 9 1/4 x 6 1/8 (23.5 x 15.6),
sheet (*Una*); 11 3/4 x 15 1/2 (29.8 x 39.8), mat
The Stratford Festival, Canada

Scene from *The Lost Leader*, Abbey Theatre, Dublin,
1937 (photo: Tanya Moiseiwitsch Collection)

Fred Johnson as Timmy the Smith and Cyril Cusack as Martin Doul in the scene, "Outside the Forge," from *The Well of the Saints*, Abbey Theatre, Dublin, 1938 (photo: Tanya Moiseiwitsch Collection)

I was invited by Hugh Hunt to come to the Abbey Theatre in Ireland. He wanted someone to design for him, but he really wanted to say what he wanted in the way of layout for the stage plan. He also wanted a certain amount to do with the color and the atmosphere. But he was very open-minded about costumes and said, "Just do what you can in the time we have." And there was very little time because when I got to Dublin I found out there was a whole other way of working. It was repertory in the truest sense. They'd pull things out of stock that had been hidden for ten years and dusted them off, and the show went on Monday—a new show every Monday. It didn't always look quite as spruce as perhaps one would wish. Hugh Hunt was on a trial basis, as I was, for three months. We tried to raise the standards a bit from the scenic angle. The acting angle of course was simply wonderful, but costumes hardly existed. The wardrobe consisted of one lady in charge of a lot of tweed coats and one or two red petticoats from the west of Ireland and after that, oh dear you had to do quite a lot of imagining. We were there for three months waiting to be told whether or not we should then go back to England. As it turned out, we both stayed there for over three years. Not bad, eh?

Scene from *Casadh an t'Súgain*, Abbey Theatre,
Dublin, 1938 (photo: Tanya Moiseiwitsch Collection)

Cyrano de Bergerac

Old Vic at the New Theatre
London, 1946

THE CURTAIN ROSE SMARTLY on the Old Vic's production of *Cyrano de Bergerac* on opening night, 24 October 1946, to reveal a remarkable ensemble of talent: Ralph Richardson in the title role, Margaret Leighton as Roxane, Michael Warre as Christian, and Alec Guinness as De Guiche, with Tyrone Guthrie directing and Tanya Moiseiwitsch designing costumes and settings. For this heroic comedy in five acts, set in 1640, the script requires locations including the hall of the Hôtel de Bourgogne, the pastry shop of Raguenu, Roxane's house with jasmine embracing its famous balcony and garden wall, a battlefield at the siege of Arras with ramparts and a distant plain, and finally, fifteen years later in Paris, a park at the Ladies of the Cross Convent, shaded by an enormous tree which slowly drops its autumn leaves. The company would have the audience believing it all, including the falling leaves in the fifth act—pages of the *Evening Standard* Moiseiwitsch had cut up and dyed in tea.

At the Old Vic, where budgets were small, design was always an invitation to innovation. Practical realities, especially in postwar 1946, meant that the designer's first task was to sift through wardrobe storage to see how many existing costumes could be used as they were, or how they could be revived. Yet what the designer lacked in production budget, she compensated for in imagination; Moiseiwitsch's vision for the production remained clear.

The director and designer had agreed to the shape, palette, and period for Edmond Rostand's romantic tale, when they decided the portraits of Franz Hals would be their point of departure. Deep browns, sepias, and toast colors were mainly chosen for the costumes of the cadets and Cyrano; blacks for the Spaniards, and in order to lend contrast, bright, eye-catching whites, creams, and golds for the flamboyant Montfleury (fig. no. 40, color plate 14) in the opening scene at the Hôtel de Bour-

gogne. Against all the frills and fluttering of this poet-actor, compare the gallant simplicity of Cyrano's inky black costume (fig. no. 41, color plate 12)—no flash, just panache: wide white cuffs, spread rolled collars, no ruffs, and, of course, the white plume. All the cadets of Gascony, plus Richardson as Cyrano, sported moustaches with Van Dyck or stiletto beards, visually to unify this brotherhood with blades in hand and ballads on the lip.

In her design for De Guiche (fig. no. 43, color plate 13), Moiseiwitsch displayed her sensitivity to costume references found in Rostand's poetic text. In the fourth act, cadets mutter among themselves, mocking their colonel's vanity as he approaches from a distance:

A CADET: He makes me weary!
ANOTHER: With his collar Of lace over his corselet—
ANOTHER: Like a ribbon Tied round a sword!
ANOTHER: Bandages for a boil On the back of his neck—
SECOND CADET: A courtier always!
ANOTHER: The Cardinal's nephew!
CARBON: None the less—a Gascon.
FIRST CADET: A counterfeit! Never you trust that man— Because we Gascons, look you, are all mad—This fellow is reasonable—nothing more Dangerous than a reasonable Gascon!
LE BRET: He looks pale.
ANOTHER: Oh, he can be hungry too, Like any other poor devil—but he wears So many jewels on that belt of his That his cramps glitter in the sun![1]

Carefully gleaning these literary cues, Moiseiwitsch incorporated them in her design. Inspired by Hals, she envisioned De Guiche as a courtierlike cavalier in a rich scarlet hue associated with the Cardinal's office. The costume is a remarkable blend of historical detail, textual accuracy, and interpretive tone.

Scheming with her director, Moiseiwitsch came up with poignant touches for even the smallest of roles, to reveal character and help unfold the tale. Her sketch for the character identified

40

41

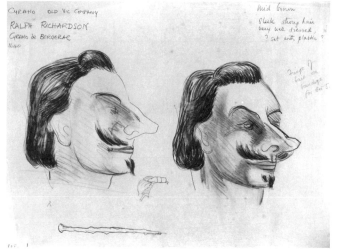

42

43

40. *Montfleury* from *Cyrano de Bergerac*, 1946, cat. no. 41

41. *Cyrano de Bergerac* from *Cyrano de Bergerac*, 1946, cat. no. 37

42. *Wig and Nose Design for Cyrano* from *Cyrano de Bergerac*, 1946, cat. no. 39

43. *De Guiche, Act 1* from *Cyrano de Bergerac*, 1946, cat. no. 40

only as "a poet" (fig. no. 44) probably communicates more information visually than the actor delivered vocally, with rolled-down stockings and frayed carpet slippers. The design, combined with Guthrie's staging and the performances of an extraordinarily talented cast, had a powerful effect, as an eyewitness to the production recorded:

> In costume and setting it had a marvelous mellow integrity of tones; the whole thing deeply romantic. It moved with amazing fluency from scene to scene and Richardson had the wind of genius in him. Margaret Leighton was a dream of a Roxane, Alec Guinness such a stylish De Guiche. But the revelation of that production was the sweep of the Guthrie direction; and its effectiveness in the crowd scenes. In the first scene of the play, in the courtyard of the Hôtel de Bourgogne, the way in which one character (Cyrano) was made to emerge as the product of his whole society till he was finally the focal point of the whole play—this was superb. And then how the whole social tide of humanity surrounding him could smoothly ebb away—to leave him alone and suddenly so approachable by the whole audience—this was the Guthrie touch.[2]

It was a touch more deeply felt because of the design. If one thinks of the proscenium stage as a frame, the designer must aid the director in creating the stage picture by providing levels or planes for such groupings, for shaping the space to suggest locale, atmosphere, mood, and time of day, and for shifting the audience's focus of attention. To achieve this in *Cyrano*, Moiseiwitsch in part looked to old-master painters, and certainly to Hals, for their use of chiaroscuro, the painterly technique of manipulating the play of light and shadow. During the fourth act, the melding of design and chiaroscuro were memorably demonstrated. The setting itself (fig. no. 47, color plate 11), acting as an interior framing device, molded the picture dramatically. Tattered shambles, a towering windmill, and a broken fence upstage divided the proscenium rec-

tangle and defined the space. The act begins just before dawn, as a smoky haze lingers on the battlefield, strewn with weapons and starving soldiers huddled around flickering camp fires. Their empty stomachs and sleepless watches have darkened their spirits. Roxane will bring food to the hungry sons of Gascony and brighten the mood. To emphasize this shift, Moiseiwitsch dressed Roxane in golden yellow, following Guthrie's suggestion that her entrance be "like the break of day," and this bright splash of color against the somber tones had an arresting visual effect. Here controlled use of color heightened a dramatic moment and allowed Guthrie to create a powerful stage picture.

All this artful illusion had to be shoe-horned into a strict budget and an even smaller backstage space. *Cyrano de Bergerac* was the third offering in the Old Vic's 1946 repertory, so that all of Moiseiwitsch's plans for setting and props needed to be stored in the severely limited wing space or concealed above the stage—hanging on batons which could be "flown in," that is, lowered onto the stage. Everything had to be stored for quick scene changes and still accommodate staging requirements of the other two productions in the rotating repertory. At the designer's first meeting with the Old Vic's management—Laurence Olivier, John Burrell, and Richardson—Moiseiwitsch and Guthrie presented a painted cardboard model of their plans for each setting (now preserved in the Theatre Museum, London). Olivier remarked, "She thinks we are doing it in the Coliseum—you don't have all the space in the world, dear."[3] With the restricted backstage facilities at the New Theatre, temporary home to the Old Vic, the plans needed major modification.

In conjunction with her fellow designers charged with creating the other two productions, *King Lear* and J. B. Priestly's *An Inspector Calls*, Moiseiwitsch juggled her plans around the Old Vic's "rep" requirements, to share what little space was available. Dimensions were refigured, alternate schemes dreamed up and plotted for their efficiency. For example, for the battle scene in act 4 of *Cyrano*, the depth of a wall stretching along part of the horizon was reduced. To save floor space in the wings, the windmill,

44

45

46

47

44. *A Poet* from *Cyrano de Bergerac*, 1946, cat. no. 36

45. *A Busybody, Act 1* from *Cyrano de Bergerac*, 1946, cat. no. 35

46. *Roxane, Act 5* from *Cyrano de Bergerac*, 1946, cat. no. 42

47. *Set Design, Act 4* from *Cyrano de Bergerac*, 1946, cat. no. 34

originally planned to be wheeled off stage on a wagon (a small platform with rollers), was altered: the arms became a flat drop-unit that could be suspended from the fly lines over the stage and flown out when no longer needed. Moiseiwitsch rethought the function of backdrops, wings, and set pieces in relation to the other shows; thanks to her resourcefulness, the actual look of *Cyrano*, as finally approved by the management, had not been compromised.

Amidst the ruins and economic hardships of postwar London, the Old Vic production brought visual delight and colorful poetic language to its audiences. Reviews glowed and a dozen critics wrote with adulation about Richardson's masterly performance, Guthrie's brilliant direction, and the romantic spell cast by Moiseiwitsch's designs, hailed as "a triumph of period atmosphere and theatrical skill."[4] A few critics grumbled over the scope of Rostand's play, Brian Hooker's translation, or Guthrie's cutting; Ivor Brown, for instance, writing for *The Observer*, faulted the play for being unsuited to the times. Nevertheless, he lauded the design of scenery and costumes as "delightful," and, impressed by Richardson's deeply felt balcony scene, confessed that "to evoke that response to romance, in these days is almost a miracle."[5]

The *Manchester Guardian* noted that the director "with the help of some magnificently romantic scenery by Tanya Moiseiwitsch, and the cooperation of the company" made a very brave showing with this handsome and popular revival. The reviewer called for "more light in scenes which do not depend on a reasonable degree of darkness," but generally praised the production's visual aspects, commenting that "the company lives up, as far as humanly possible, to the picturesqueness of Rostand's dreams of romantic France."[6] One cynical critic, no fan of the playwright, called the script "a piece of theatrical hooey that always works.... It is the tragedy of a chocolate box lid, but what charm it has!" He concluded that by the time the director and his team "have put their imaginations into it, we are almost moved to tears."[7]

Moiseiwitsch created a dozen productions for the Old Vic during the 1940s. Each demonstrated her genuine skill and artistic development in period design; each was a masterpiece of visual interpretation based on historical research, though none was more fondly remembered than this *Cyrano de Bergerac*. In 1948, Audrey Williamson recalled the poignant details of Moiseiwitsch's contribution to the success of *Cyrano*: "Her carved oak and darkening candlelight of the theater scene, her windmill with battered wings against the leaden sky, and her beautiful last scene of falling leaves and opaque fog and melancholy, were the highest creative achievements of recent stage design."[8]

NOTES

1. Edmond Rostand, *Cyrano de Bergerac* (New York: Bantam, 1982), 137.

2. James Forsyth, *Tyrone Guthrie, A Biography* (London: Hamish Hamilton, 1976), 199.

3. Tanya Moiseiwitsch, interview with the author, Stratford, Ontario, 24 June 1992.

4. Audrey Williamson, *Old Vic Drama* (London: Rockcliff, 1948), 203.

5. Ivor Brown, "Come Fly with Me," *The Observer*, n.d. This and the two subsequently cited reviews are from the Old Vic Press Clippings Book, Theatre Museum, London.

6. "Cyrano de Bergerac," *Manchester Guardian*, n.d.

7. "Richardson Has Triumph," *Rialto*, 27 October 1946.

8. Williamson, *Old Vic Drama*, 203.

CYRANO DE BERGERAC

Old Vic Theatre Company at the New Theatre
London, 1946
Directed by Tyrone Guthrie

34
Set Design, Act 4
Pencil, watercolor, gouache on paper,
11 x 14 15/16 (27.9 x 37.9)
Tanya Moiseiwitsch Collection

35
A Busybody, Act 1 (John Garley)
Pencil, watercolor on paper,
14 15/16 x 9 13/16 (37.9 x 24.9)
Tanya Moiseiwitsch Collection

36
A Poet (George Relph)
Pencil, watercolor on paper,
13 3/4 x 9 7/8 (34.9 x 24)
Tanya Moiseiwitsch Collection

37
Cyrano de Bergerac (Ralph Richardson)
Pencil, watercolor on paper,
13 13/16 x 9 5/16 (35.1 x 23.6), image
Tanya Moiseiwitsch Collection

38*
Cyrano
Pencil, gouache, watercolor on paper,
15 x 10 (38.1 x 25.5)
Tanya Moiseiwitsch Collection

39
Wig and Nose Design for Cyrano
Pencil, watercolor on paper,
14 1/16 x 19 7/8 (35.7 x 50.5)
Tanya Moiseiwitsch Collection

40
De Guiche, Act 1 (Alec Guinness)
Pencil, watercolor, fabric swatches on paper,
14 15/16 x 10 (37.9 x 25.5)
Tanya Moiseiwitsch Collection

41
Montfleury (George Rose)
Pencil, watercolor on paper,
14 11/16 x 9 5/8 (37.3 x 24.4), image
Tanya Moiseiwitsch Collection

42
Roxane, Act 5 (Margaret Leighton)
Pencil, watercolor on paper,
15 x 9 13/16 (38.1 x 24.9)
Tanya Moiseiwitsch Collection

Michael Warre as Christian and Ralph Richardson as Cyrano in *Cyrano de Bergerac*, Old Vic Theatre Company at the New Theatre, London, 1946 (photo: John Vickers, London)

We worked at Cyrano with the idea of fitting it into the Old Vic's repertory program. I was told that there would be four or five plays on the stage, which did not have much wing space. It was a case of trying to find storage space in the wings when your play wasn't on the stage, and King Lear or something else was taking place. We didn't take too much note of the measurements and the first set of models that was presented, which Guthrie and I thought were pretty ingenious in scene change, to Lawrence Olivier, Ralph Richardson, and John Burrell. They looked at the model rather quietly and one of them, I think it was Olivier, said, "Does she think we're doing this at the Coliseum?" And, well no, I didn't think that, it was the New Theatre stage, I've got the measurements and everything. And they said, "Yes, but it's in repertory you know, we're doing other plays as well," and I said "Yes, I do know." "Well, it's much too big—it won't do. And you must think again." Tony Guthrie wasn't used to being told, "you must think again," but he said, "Yes, well of course we will try and accommodate a bit, we don't want to be selfish and take up too much room." And Larry said, "Well it isn't only when it's on the stage that it's too big, it's when it's off stage." Very practical. That was the beginning of a series of re-thinks which went on for several days and nights with assistance from a wonderful modelmaker, Dinah Greet, who was employed by the Old Vic at that time. She said, "I'll do anything for Guthrie, so let's get on with it." We changed it, and changed it, and changed it until it was eventually accepted. It did work and we fit it in with all of the plays.

Margaret Leighton as Roxane, Michael Warre as Christian and Ralph Richardson as Cyrano in the balcony scene, *Cyrano de Bergerac*, Old Vic Theatre Company at the New Theatre, London, 1946 (photo: John Vickers, London)

Peter Grimes

Royal Opera House, Covent Garden
London, 1947

FOR THE ROYAL OPERA HOUSE, Covent Garden, Tanya Moiseiwitsch and Tyrone Guthrie were chosen to design and direct a new production of Benjamin Britten's *Peter Grimes* in 1947. Although Guthrie admired the first production of the opera just two years earlier at Sadler's Wells, with its "rather realistic sets and some attempt at intimacy in the acting," he felt that the vast dimensions of Covent Garden required a different approach. "The majestic sweep of the score, the evocation of the sea and its ineluctable influence on the destiny of the characters could be better interpreted on a simpler, more spacious setting" that utilized the entire width and depth of the Covent Garden stage. Guthrie did not share Britten's preference for a naturalistic staging of the opera, but aimed instead for "boldly abstract expressions of atmosphere and emotion...expressions of a far-reaching poetic imagination."[1] He and Moiseiwitsch worked together to create a setting that manifested the spirit of the score on the Covent Garden stage.

Moiseiwitsch's two sets for the production captured the director's point of view. The original main setting called for the village, church, moot hall, shops, and streets—an exercise in realism. But Moiseiwitsch rejected all this for a great wooden pier stretching endlessly back into the gloomy haze, with a confusion of fishing tackle in the foreground and nets hung out to dry on the receding pilings (fig. no. 48). Transferring the action in this way from the borough to the shore freed the designer from having to depict each location in the town. The shift also succeeded, as an unidentified writer for *Musical Opinion* noted, "in suggesting the foreshore as the hub of the community where nets are mended, meetings held, dances take place and where fogs and storms are most closely apprehended."[2]

The single set piece, painted and dry-brushed to simulate rugged timbers, provided stairs and various levels for staging the

48. *Set Design* from *Peter Grimes*, 1947, cat. no. 43 (photo: Collections of the Theatre Museum. By courtesy of the Board of Trustees of the Victoria and Albert Museum, London)

49. *Design for Interlude Cloth* from *Peter Grimes*, 1947, cat. no. 45 (photo: Collections of the Theatre Museum. By courtesy of the Board of Trustees of the Victoria and Albert Museum, London)

crowd scene, while affording the singers a clear view of the conductor's downbeat. For the opening moot hall trail scene, which introduced characters and their musical themes, each principal simply rose in a stabbing beam of light from his or her location on the pier, or "sea-side" as the designer referred to the configuration of stairs and platforms. Rather than using actual doors for the pub scene, Moiseiwitsch planned a shaft of light, streaming in from the wings, which would widen, then narrow again to suggest the opening and closing of the pub door somewhere off stage. The "horizon cloth," lighting, and fog effects enhanced the magnitude of the drama. "Tanya Moiseiwitsch is determined," commented Desmond Shawn-Taylor for *The Statesman*, "that we shall feel the full impact of the elements—fog, lashing gale, [and] the vast Anglian sky."[3]

The setting for act 2, scene 2 included a low fence on the edge of a cliff which extended from downstage right to down left then swept up the proscenium arch. Serving as an interior frame and suggesting the height of the cliff, the fence also provided a foreground for the audience to look beyond, emphasizing distance and space. Center stage, on an elevated platform, covered with sails and fishing nets, was Grimes's shed (fig. no. 50, color plate 16). The tiny refuge, with beams like the ribs of a rowboat, was furnished with ropes and kegs. The setting served the action, especially when the ill-fated boy apprentice slithered over the precipice with a shriek to his death. Moiseiwitsch's setting added "another whole dimension to the opera," wrote the same critic for *The Statesman*. "Peter now dreams of happiness on the cliff edge with his eyes on the distant horizon, an effect that brings out all the poetry of this lovely passage." Thanks to the stage design, Shawn-Taylor continued, "the fundamental idea of the work—the conflict in rough and pitiless surroundings, of the mob and individual, takes on a clearer and more ominous meaning."[4]

Eric Bloom, writing for the *Birmingham Gazette*, declared a "triumph in stagecraft.... Tanya Moiseiwitsch's settings have not only a beauty of their own but seem to carry the very swell and

50. *Set Design for Grimes's Hut* from *Peter Grimes*, 1947, cat. no. 44

51. *Ned Keene* from *Peter Grimes*, 1947, cat. no. 49

52. *Niece II, Act 3* from *Peter Grimes*, 1947, cat. no. 50

53. *Mrs. Sedley* from *Peter Grimes*, 1947, cat. no. 52

climate of the Suffolk coast."[5] However, critical reactions to the stage sets were mixed. There were requests for a return to the realistic details of the borough. The *Manchester Guardian* struck a familiar chord: "What a pity that in this superb production we are not allowed to see the church, the congregation, and the parson."[6] Apparently not all critics were prepared to be cut adrift from the realism of the first production. Moiseiwitsch's simple and spacious designs illuminated Guthrie's interpretation of the opera, centering on the fate of Grimes and the elemental forces of man and nature, in a highly dynamic atmosphere. The sparse set created an impression of immensity and allowed the stage picture to grow out of crowd movements and character groupings rather than painted flats or decorations.

Atmosphere and dramatic clarity were enhanced by Moiseiwitsch's choice of historical period and use of color. The opera was derived, albeit distantly, from George Crabbe's lengthy poem, "The Borough," set about 1790. When it came to a question of placing the opera in an epoch, the designer and her director emphasized the time period of 1830. By simplifying their style the costumes could be more direct in communicating occupation, mood, and social station. Ned Keene (fig. no. 51, color plate 17) is clearly identifiable as a gent of some means, with vest, top hat, walking stick, and a hint of prospering self-sufficiency. With the change in period, the story-telling quality of the stage picture becomes clearer, more comprehensible for a contemporary audience, which was, indeed, one of the goals of the English opera movement of the late 1940s.

The grim mood, and its prevailing sense of tragic outcome, was supported by the restrained palette of blues, grays, silvers, and blacks. The *Niece II* sketch (fig. no. 52, color plate 18) notes the garment is to be dyed to bring it into the same color family of the other niece's costumes, thereby complementing Auntie's colors. The widow in black, Mrs. Sedley (fig. no. 53), is suitably costumed, and, with the addition of a head scarf for act 2's church scene, piously proper. The social conventions and harsh realities

54

55

56

57

54. *The Rector* from *Peter Grimes*, 1947, cat. no. 51

55. *Auntie, Act 2, Scene 1* from *Peter Grimes*, 1947, cat. no. 46 (photo: Collections of the Theatre Museum. By courtesy of the Board of Trustees of the Victoria and Albert Museum, London)

56. *Ellen Orford* from *Peter Grimes*, 1947, cat. no. 47

57. *Chorus: Fisherman* from *Peter Grimes*, 1947, cat. no. 48 (photo: Collections of the Theatre Museum. By courtesy of the Board of Trustees of the Victoria and Albert Museum, London)

of this village are reflected in the strictly controlled sober use of color. The designer's delicious sense of irony is revealed in the clothes and makeup for the rector (fig. no. 54), which she created to "look like Rev. George Crabbe" according to the artist's notes. In reality, Crabbe took the holy orders of the church as a means of supporting himself as a poet and buying himself time to write. Unlike Peter Grimes, he was a loner who surrendered to convention, or at least made peace with it. The borough community he wrote about was Aldeburgh on England's Suffolk coast, which is also the home of Britten. Did the actual location serve to inspire Moiseiwitsch's choice of color for the stage design? Not really, it was Guthrie's gray tabby. "It's a place that knows slate skies, pounding waves, deadly storms, and a restless sea...of course the look (of *Peter Grimes*) is severe, that's Aldeburgh," reminisced the designer.

If a principle of design for the stage is not only to support the action, but to become integral to its expression, then Moiseiwitsch's design for *Peter Grimes* received its highest accolade, from the critic who wrote, "it's all very impressive and elemental ...a visual counterpart of Britten's vivid music."[7] Following such a remarkable introduction to the operatic stage,[8] Moiseiwitsch would continue to design for the opera for the next four decades for *The Beggar's Opera*, Aldeburgh Festival; *Lady Rohesia*, Sadler's Wells; *Don Giovanni*, Covent Garden; *The Barber of Seville*, Phoenix Opera, Brighton Festival; *The Voyage of Edgar Allen Poe*, Minnesota Opera Company; and *Rigoletto* and *La Traviata*, Metropolitan Opera. For the Metropolitan Opera Company's first season at Lincoln Center in 1966, she once again collaborated with Guthrie, to create yet another new production of *Peter Grimes*, featuring Jon Vickers, which established Britten's twentieth-century masterpiece in the Met's permanent repertory.

NOTES

1. Tyrone Guthrie, *A Life in the Theatre* (New York: McGraw Hill Book Company, Inc., 1959), 252.

2. *Musical Opinion*, January 1948. This and all subsequently cited reviews of *Peter Grimes* are collected in the Press Clipping Book, Covent Garden Archives, London.

3. Desmond Shawn-Taylor, *The Statesman*, 14 November 1947. The dramatic atmosphere was curiously amplified on opening night, when a thick London fog crept into the Royal Opera House and mixed with the stage effect, to the delight of the audience and the chagrin of the singers.

4. Ibid.

5. Eric Bloom, "World of Music," *Birmingham Gazette*, 15 December 1947.

6. *Manchester Guardian*, 12 November 1947.

7. Shawn-Taylor, *The Statesman*.

8. The Guthrie-Moiseiwitsch production of *Peter Grimes* continued in the Covent Garden repertory until 17 February 1950. *Opera* erroneously reported that "in 1953, after an absence of five years, *Grimes* returned to the Opera House." It was in fact a three-year absence. Nevertheless, the production "with Moiseiwitsch's settings (slightly adapted by Roger Ramsdell) and her original costumes remained in the repertory on and off until 1971, clocking up 63 performances—an average of two and one quarter a season" (*Opera* 26 [September 1975]: 890–95). Photographs indicate modifications to the original setting: a run of flats topped with contour board edges depicting shops and houses that extend upstage of the pier heighten the illusion of depth.

PETER GRIMES

Royal Opera House, Covent Garden
London, 1947
Directed by Tyrone Guthrie

43
Set Design
Watercolor, pencil, crayon on paper,
24 11/16 x 28 3/16 (62.6 x 71.6), image
From the Collections of the Theatre Museum.
By courtesy of the Board of Trustees of the
Victoria and Albert Museum, London

44
Set Design for Grimes's Hut
Pencil, pen and ink, wash, body color on paper,
13 7/8 x 19 (35.3 x 48.3), image
Tanya Moiseiwitsch Collection

45
Design for Interlude Cloth
Pen and ink, pencil, chalk, gouache, watercolor
on paper, 16 3/4 x 23 7/16 (42.5 x 59.5), image
From the Collections of the Theatre Museum.
By courtesy of the Board of Trustees of the
Victoria and Albert Museum, London

46
Auntie, Act 2, Scene 1 (Edith Coates)
Pencil, pen and ink, watercolor on paper,
14 7/8 x 12 (38.2 x 30.5), image
From the Collections of the Theatre Museum.
By courtesy of the Board of Trustees of the
Victoria and Albert Museum, London

47
Ellen Orford (Joan Cross)
Pencil, pen and brush and ink, watercolor on
paper, 15 1/8 x 11 3/4 (38.5 x 29.8)
Tanya Moiseiwitsch Collection

48
Chorus: Fisherman
Watercolor, wash, pencil, ink on paper,
15 x 11 1/2 (37.5 x 28.5), image
From the Collections of the Theatre Museum.
By courtesy of the Board of Trustees of the Vic-
toria and Albert Museum, London

49
Ned Keene (Grahame Clifford)
Pencil, pen and brush and ink, watercolor on
paper, 15 1/8 x 11 5/8 (38.5 x 29.4)
Tanya Moiseiwitsch Collection

50
Niece II, Act 3
Pencil, pen and ink, watercolor on paper,
15 5/16 x 12 1/8 (48.9 x 30.8)
Tanya Moiseiwitsch Collection

51
The Rector (David Tree)
Pencil, pen and brush and ink, watercolor,
gouache on paper, 15 1/8 x 12 3/16 (38.5 x 31)
Tanya Moiseiwitsch Collection

52
Mrs. Sedley (Constance Shacklock)
Pencil, pen and ink, watercolor on paper,
15 x 10 3/8 (38.1 x 26.3)
Tanya Moiseiwitsch Collection

Peter Pears as Peter Grimes and Joan
Cross as Ellen Orford in *Peter Grimes*,
Royal Opera House, Covent Garden,
London, 1947 (photo: Angus McBean.
Harvard Theatre Collection)

Opposite: The Borough Company
in act 1, scene 1 of *Peter Grimes*,
Royal Opera House, Covent Garden,
London, 1947 (photo: Angus McBean.
Harvard Theatre Collection)

But, Peter Grimes *wasn't pretty by any means, it was very stark and that caused problems too because in later years Benjamin Britten wanted it "fussied up" to be made more like the village that he knew and loved. I don't know if he didn't approve of the idea of the pier, or just the whole idea of the sea being the hero of the piece perhaps just as much. Well, it was Grimes versus the sea to Guthrie, who saw it as a great monumental work. Ben still saw it as a little village and he wanted the little village expressed more visually, not just a door shutting or something. Anyway, in the end, it was altered quite considerably. But we learned our lesson on that, because when we did it again at the Met, about twenty years later, we spent a day in Aldeburgh showing Mr. Britten—Sir Britten—what we had thought up. This time he approved every single thing—because we knew what he wanted. And it was fantastic. Of course we didn't have the real fog at the Met, we had a fog machine they got from Hollywood which they were told didn't upset people's voices at all and they didn't mind a bit. But—did they ever mind!* Oooooh!

Hubert Norville as Bob Boles and Muriel Burnett
and Blanche Turner as the nieces in *Peter Grimes*,
Royal Opera House, Covent Garden, London, 1947
(photo: Angus McBean. Harvard Theatre Collection)

The History Cycle
Shakespeare Memorial Theatre
Stratford-upon-Avon, 1951

58. *Frontispiece of the Set Design* from *The History Cycle*, 1951, collection of Mr. and Mrs. Desmond Hall, not in exhibition (photo: Shakespeare Centre Library, Stratford-upon-Avon)

"THE RESOURCES OF the Shakespeare Memorial Theatre and the occasion of the Festival of Britain combined in 1951 to bring about a rare theatrical phenomenon—the performance in sequence of Shakespeare's four history plays, *Richard II*, *Henry IV, Parts I and II*, and *Henry V*," wrote Anthony Quayle, actor and artistic director of the Shakespeare Memorial Theatre. Although Quayle cited records indicating that the plays had been performed as a cycle at Stratford by Sir Frank Benson's company in 1905, he could not determine beyond that whether such an event had been staged since Shakespeare's day. The cycle's directors—John Kidd, Quayle, and Michael Redgrave—and designer Tanya Moiseiwitsch "never doubted that the plays were written as one great tetralogy;" indeed, their "full power and meaning only become apparent when [they were] treated as a whole."[1]

The goal of unifying that which had long been divided could only be realized with a set and production design that could serve all four plays; different settings for each play would have destroyed the very unity for which Quayle and his collaborators were striving. To devise such a set was an enormous challenge for Moiseiwitsch, for it had to be "capable of embracing court and tavern, shire and city, indoor and out-of-door." Quayle realized that the set had to suggest "the lists at Coventry and the quay-side at Southampton, it had to house the rebels in their barn before the battle of Shrewsbury, and the dying Bolingbroke in the Jerusalem chamber; and ... it had to suggest the 'wooden O' [Shakespeare's Globe Theatre] of *Henry V*." The designer rose to this exceptional task: "All these problems," stated Quayle, "Miss Moiseiwitsch solved triumphantly."[2]

How did Moiseiwitsch create a permanent set that served all four productions and gave the cycle stylistic continuity? In an essay in *Shakespeare Survey*, Richard David stated that her set

59. *John of Gaunt, Scenes 1 and 3* from *Richard II*, 1951, cat. no. 54 (photo: Shakespeare Centre Library, Stratford-upon-Avon)

60. *Queen to Richard, Scenes 12 and 14 from Richard II,* 1951, cat. no. 55 (photo: Shakespeare Centre Library, Stratford-upon-Avon)

61. *Acolyte, Scene 14 from Henry IV, Part I,* 1951, cat. no. 56 (photo: Shakespeare Centre Library, Stratford-upon-Avon)

was modeled on the Elizabethan public stage, "a bulky scaffolding with a canopied balcony…and stairs curving down either side. To the left a throne, to the right a penthouse flanked the stage, and the whole was framed in draperies of smoky blue." David also pointed out that "the space beneath the balcony could be closed by heavy stable doors; when these were open it afforded not so much an inner stage as an antechamber to the stage, a half-way house, on-stage and off-stage."[3] While this description is accurate, the reference to the Elizabethan stage as the source for the design may be less so. The quest to discover the definitive Elizabethan playhouse setting has long been a passionate scholarly pursuit of theater historians. Many have offered conjectural models, true, but for Moiseiwitsch, this set was also derived from years of practical experience and, quite surprisingly, from a medieval French drawing reproduced in a book handed to her by her close collaborator and assistant for these productions, Alix Stone.

In the medieval era, royalty often viewed jousts and tourneys from specially constructed viewing galleries. Built of timber, the viewing stand was a crude structure of scaffolding beams and flooring, but when hung with garlands, banners, or tapestries, the simple edifice took on a regal air. Inspired by the tournament viewing stand, Moiseiwitsch added asymmetry to its basic design to increase its visual appeal; with stair units built onto the structure both above and below, she offered playing space for individuals or large groups. The permanent setting could be as common as the world of the inn, or as formal as the court with all its pomp and pageantry at coronation. Not a pedantic reconstruction, Moiseiwitsch's set served as a brilliant foundation for the whole historical cycle, supporting the action, even accelerating it.

In designing *Henry VIII* for the Shakespeare Memorial Theatre in 1949, Moiseiwitsch had begun to see how properties could replace scenery with swift changes of a few stools, chairs, and tables. She found a visual parallel to the Bard's economy of words to indicate place and time. For the history plays, avoiding a stage full of painted scenery which required time to shift with every change of locale, she gave "a habitation and a name" often with only a single significant prop. *Richard II* began with the fewest props; as the cycle progressed, more were used to indicate more locales. "A high settle for Cheapside, a wattle fence for the Gloucestershire orchard, a monkish chair for the Archbishop's palace at York," a prop became a potent symbol for atmosphere as well as for a particular site. The stage, as David observed in *Shakespeare Survey*, seemed "protean, everything and nothing, a delight to the eye and invisible . . . less a formal framework for action than a space of apparently infinite extension and possibility into which any action fitted naturally."[4]

Looking back on the productions, Moiseiwitsch remembered that her design concept was not immediately workable for each play's director. "Are we flouting the convention if . . . ?" was a phrase that sometimes preceded a suggestion for extra tables, or a pub sign announcing "Boar's Head," or some rounded straw skeps for bees to indicate the countryside. Action was the axiom— that is, if a property was actually used in the scene, integral to the stage business, then Moiseiwitsch most likely accepted the suggestion; a problem arose only when the prop requested was nothing more than a decoration. A proposal for a backdrop for a scene, however, was totally incongruous with the design premise. For Moiseiwitsch, a backdrop would have represented a retreat to the painted illusions of the proscenium stage. Her solution in *Henry V* was a huge billowing canopy which softened the permanent set's outline while providing the atmosphere of a tent.

The sheer economic and organizational challenge in costuming the complete tetralogy was formidable. Moiseiwitsch attacked the problem with her customary down-to-earth approach. With the directors, she fixed the period of 1390 for *Richard II* and proceeded chronologically for the other three plays. While overseeing the entire project, she concentrated on costuming the English characters and determined a color scheme which divided the world of the court from that of the inn (fig. nos. 62–65, color plates 20, 21). She conceived the court costumes in reds, yellows, and oranges, and the clothing of common citizens and innspeople in browns,

62. *Bardolph, Armed* from *Henry IV, Part I*, 1951, cat. no. 57 (photo: Shakespeare Centre Library, Stratford-upon-Avon)

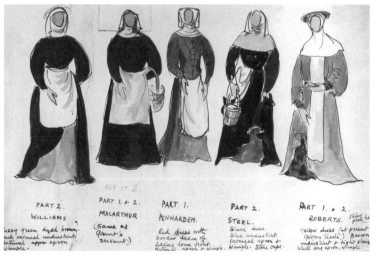

63

63. *Earl of Douglas, Scenes 11, 13, 16, 17, and 18* from *Henry IV, Part I*, 1951, cat. no. 58 (photo: Shakespeare Centre Library, Stratford-upon-Avon)

64. *Inn Types and Citizens: The Sheriff and Men, Scenes 7 and 10* from *Henry IV, Part I*, 1951, cat. no. 59 (photo: Shakespeare Centre Library, Stratford-upon-Avon)

65. *Inn Types and Citizens: Women* from *Henry IV, Part I*, 1951, cat. no. 60 (photo: Shakespeare Centre Library, Stratford-upon-Avon)

66. *Fang and Snare* from *Henry IV, Part II*, 1951, cat. no. 61 (photo: Shakespeare Centre Library, Stratford-upon-Avon)

67. *Pistol* from *Henry IV, Part II*, 1951, cat. no. 62 (photo: Shakespeare Centre Library, Stratford-upon-Avon)

68. *Rumour after Casting Cloak Away* from *Henry IV, Part II*, 1951, cat. no. 63 (photo: Shakespeare Centre Library, Stratford-upon-Avon)

mustards, blacks, grays, and greens. Assisting her, Stone, who excelled at costume sketches of armored soldiers and in fabricating their theatrical facsimile, was assigned the French army. Their blue uniforms, clearly distinct from the contrasting red attire of the English, were historically accurate. Because Stone was an invaluable resource on colors and symbology, the all-important language of heraldry—used to identify innumerable dukes with their various fiefdoms and counties—was also delegated to her.

Comparing the 230 costume plates for the cycle reveals that Moiseiwitsch's warm and cool palettes helped to distinguish individuals and groups of characters, while her selection of materials such as raffia, straw, and coarsely woven fabrics reflected social and economic rank (fig. no. 69). Breaking down fabrics using dyes and scenic paints to age, discolor, and weather the costumes made

them appear as natural and realistic clothing. In fact, according to David in *Shakespeare Survey*, the greatest virtue of Moiseiwitsch's costumes for these productions "was that they sat on their wearers with an every-day comfortableness and seemed inevitable—a powerful strengthening of the illusion of the historicity."[5]

Integrating costumes, properties, and settings for the history plays, weaving them together stylistically yielded a rich panoramic theatrical tapestry. On a permanent setting, the arrangement of stairs, gallery, and study gave balance to stage pictures. Thrusting the study and the gallery forward toward the audience improved sight lines and gave new dominance to the gallery above as a staging area. The opening below the gallery allowed the study to be used as an antechamber where characters could enter and be only partially seen. Stairways and landings in both settings proved to

70

69. *First Gardener, Scene 12* from *Richard II*, 1951, cat. no. 53 (photo: Shakespeare Centre Library, Stratford-upon-Avon)

70. *King Henry V, Scene 23* from *Henry V*, 1951, cat. no. 64 (photo: Shakespeare Centre Library, Stratford-upon-Avon)

be natural playing spaces, and the various levels lent diversity to the stage pictures, while steps helped solve masking problems on the forestage. The color of the permanent set served as a generalized background because it affected subsequent choices in costume colors. Moiseiwitsch's rich warm wooden tones were dark and serviceable. Simple shifting of properties for scene changes preserved the plays' continuity and rhythm while color and texture in costumes created contrasting atmospheres and underscored dramatic moments.

Ironically, the biggest single obstacle—the proscenium arch—was a fixed feature of the very playhouse designed for Shakespearean productions, the Shakespeare Memorial Theatre at Stratford-upon-Avon. When Moiseiwitsch and Tyrone Guthrie had collaborated at Stratford on *Henry VIII*, the designer recalled, "he wanted to believe that there was not a proscenium in this theater that was built entirely for Shakespeare." Moiseiwitsch explained, "It wasn't a real proscenium arch, but it divided the stage picture from the rows of seats in a straight line. And Quayle felt the same," she continued, "he too wanted to ignore it. But it was very hard to ignore. It was a basic part of the building; the formation of seats were, and more or less still are, like an opera house."[6] Tacking on a fifteen-foot forestage might push the actor toward the audience but could never place him or her in the intimate spa-

tial relationship with the whole audience that the Elizabethan actor had enjoyed; the configuration of the building prohibited it. The actor could not be encircled by the spectators, because they always confronted the stage at the Shakespeare Memorial Theatre.

This arrangement was a source of great frustration for Moiseiwitsch. "We tried to ignore the proscenium," she remembered, "and tried every device known to man to by-pass it, and cover it up, and say it wasn't there."[7] Her practical solution was to extend the setting along the walls of the theater to hide the arch, using a throne and penthouse, swags of curtains, and stylized banners of cheesecloth, even a trellis—anything to carry the eye beyond the frame. These camouflage attempts, however, could not conceal the uncongenial architecture, and for the designer, the results were never completely satisfying.

Her experiments with the history plays convinced Moiseiwitsch that Shakespeare could be produced on a simple wooden permanent set, with striking costumes and a few properties to stimulate the viewer's imagination. The productions demonstrated to her that the proscenium arch and Elizabethan stage convention were irreconcilable. How she solved this problem is the story of the Festival Theatre in Stratford, Ontario. All her work in the theater, especially with Guthrie, was preparing her for that solution.

NOTES

1. Anthony Quayle, quoted in J. Dover Wilson and T. C. Worsley, *Shakespeare's Histories at Stratford* (London: Max Reinhart, 1952), vii.

2. Ibid., ix.

3. Richard David, "Shakespeare's History Plays: Epic or Drama," in *Shakespeare Survey*, vol. 6, edited by Allardyce Nicoll (Cambridge: Cambridge at the University Press, 1953), 129.

4. Ibid., 130.

5. Ibid.

6. Tanya Moiseiwitsch, interviewed by James Wallace, "The First Ten Years of Scenic Design at the Guthrie Theater," Ph.D. diss., University of Minnesota, 1975, 2:249, 243. Hereafter cited as "Wallace interview."

Guthrie in particular disliked the red-brick monument to Shakespeare, built without regard to the staging conventions of the Bard's plays. In fact, he once suggested that Quayle construct a theater on the river bank next to the Dirty Duck, a favorite pub of Stratford actors. Quayle objected, "But, Tony, we can't have two theaters here, what would I do with the Memorial Theatre?" "Push it into the river," came the reply. (James Forsyth, *Tyrone Guthrie, A Biography* [London: Hamish Hamilton, 1976], 209.) Moiseiwitsch recalled the same exchange during an interview with the author.

7. Wallace interview, 2:249.

THE HISTORY CYCLE

Shakespeare Memorial Theatre
Stratford-upon-Avon, 1951

Richard II
Directed by Anthony Quayle
Design assisted by Alix Stone

53
First Gardener, Scene 12 (Godfrey Bond)
Pen and ink, watercolor on paper,
14 13/16 x 11 1/2 (36.2 x 27.2)
Shakespeare Centre Library, Stratford-upon-
Avon

54
John of Gaunt, Scenes 1 and 3 (Hugh Griffith)
Pen and ink, watercolor, fabric swatches on
paper, 16 1/8 x 11 1/2 (41 x 29)
Shakespeare Centre Library, Stratford-upon-
Avon

55
Queen to Richard, Scenes 12 and 14
(Heather Stannard and Michael Redgrave)
Pen and ink, wash on paper,
15 x 10 5/8 (38.1 x 26.3)
Shakespeare Centre Library, Stratford-upon-
Avon

Henry IV, Part I
Directed by Anthony Quayle and John Kidd
Design assisted by Alix Stone

56
Acolyte, Scene 14
Pen and ink, wash on paper, 16 x 11 9/16
(40.7 x 29.5)
Shakespeare Centre Library, Stratford-upon-
Avon

57
Bardolph, Armed (Michael Bates)
Pen and ink, watercolor on paper,
18 7/8 x 9 7/8 (48 x 25.1)
Shakespeare Centre Library, Stratford-upon-
Avon

58
Earl of Douglas, Scenes 11, 13, 16, 17, and 18
(Phillip Morant)
Pen and ink, watercolor, fabric swatch on
paper, 17 13/16 x 10 7/8 (45.2 x 27.6)
Shakespeare Centre Library, Stratford-upon-
Avon

59
*Inn Types and Citizens: The Sheriff and Men,
Scenes 7 and 10*
Pen and ink, watercolor on paper,
9 15/16 x 11 5/8 (25.2 x 29.5)
Shakespeare Centre Library, Stratford-upon-
Avon

60
Inn Types and Citizens: Women
(Sybil Williams, Joan MacArthur, Heather
Penwarden, Marjorie Steel, Rachel Roberts)
Pen and ink, watercolor on paper,
8 11/16 x 13 3/16 (22 x 33.5)
Shakespeare Centre Library, Stratford-upon-
Avon

Henry IV, Part II
Directed by Michael Redgrave
Design assisted by Alix Stone

61
Fang and Snare (Edward Atienza and
Peter Henchie)
Pen and ink, watercolor on paper,
19 3/4 x 13 1/4 (50.1 x 33.7)
Shakespeare Centre Library, Stratford-upon-
Avon

62
Pistol (Richard Wordsworth)
Pen and ink, watercolor, collage on paper,
20 1/16 x 14 3/8 (51 x 36.5)
Shakespeare Centre Library, Stratford-upon-
Avon

63
Rumour after Casting Cloak Away
(William Squire)
Pen and ink, watercolor on paper,
17 15/16 x 12 7/8 (45.4 x 32.6)
Shakespeare Centre Library, Stratford-upon-
Avon

Henry V
Directed by Anthony Quayle
Design assisted by Alix Stone

64
King Henry V, Scene 23 (Richard Burton)
Pen and ink, watercolor on paper,
19 5/16 x 13 3/8 (49 x 34)
Shakespeare Centre Library, Stratford-upon-
Avon

Heather Stannard as the Queen; Heather Penwarden, Rachel Roberts, and Marjorie Steel as Ladies-in-Waiting; and Godfrey Bond and Edward Atienza as Gardeners in act 3, scene 4 of *Richard II*, Shakespeare Memorial Theatre, Stratford-upon-Avon, 1951 (photo: Angus McBean. Harvard Theatre Collection)

Anthony Quayle, who was in charge at Stratford-upon-Avon at that time, dreamt up the idea for staging the history cycle. He thought that it was time that these Shakespearean history plays were linked together as one unit. Progressively one would see what happened, from Richard II to Henry V. Now, of course, everybody's doing it, and they even do six plays in a row when four were quite enough. It took an entire season to open, they didn't open four nights running, and they were spaced.

Right from the start it was planned to have a permanent set, which looked as though it was timber—because in those days you didn't mind cutting down trees. There was a timbered asymmetrical open space upstairs and downstairs and an uneven staircase on both sides. There was a place for the throne which could also become Falstaff's chair in the pub, or, if an ermine mantle wasn't flung over it, it was just a plain wooden kitchen chair. Scenic elements were very sparse. We were quite strict about it. Some members of the audience were used to more scenery but didn't get it. Instead, they got a scene which changed every five minutes with actors entering and exiting holding banners. The actors were wonderful and stalwart. They used to put on elaborate makeup, but they were never really seen because they were always behind a banner.

Rosalind Atkinson as Mistress Quickly, Edward
Atienza as Fang, Peter Henchie as Snare, Anthony
Quayle as Falstaff, and Michael Bates as Bardolph
in act 2, scene 1 of *Henry IV, Part II*, Shakespeare
Memorial Theatre, Stratford-upon-Avon, 1951
(photo: Angus McBean. Harvard Theatre Collection)

The company with Richard Burton as Henry V
and Anthony Quayle as Falstaff in act 5, scene 5 of
Henry IV, Part II, Shakespeare Memorial Theatre,
Stratford-upon-Avon, 1951 (photo: Angus McBean.
Harvard Theatre Collection)

Richard III

Stratford Festival Theatre
Ontario, 1953

The trumpeters at the entrance to the Festival tent have blown the last fanfare, to bring the stragglers to their seats; the cannon which is fired before each performance has sounded; the curtains which close the entrances to the amphitheater have been drawn, and fifteen hundred people wait. The lights on the acting area rise quickly to full and there, not hastily, yet promptly, is Richard, Duke of Gloucester, coming slowly toward us, on the topmost balcony. He does not pretend that we are not there; he does not speak quietly, as though to himself: loudly, clearly, he speaks to us, after a long, considering look.[1]

"NOW IS THE WINTER of our discontent made glorious summer by this sun of York . . . . " These first moments of *Richard III*, opening at the Stratford Festival on 13 July 1953, marked the birth of a truly unique theatrical adventure and the realization of a long-held dream. The playwright's words "made glorious" provide a perfectly apt description of Moiseiwitsch's design, not only of the production's costumes and properties, but the very stage itself, where the action now unfolded.

It is difficult to comprehend the enormity of the task that had faced Moiseiwitsch, director Tyrone Guthrie, and their collaborators that spring of 1953 as they prepared for *Richard III* and for *All's Well That Ends Well*, which would play in repertory. There were scores of costumes to create, cut, fit, sew, and finish. The logistics of producing two plays simultaneously, coordinating not only costumes but properties, wigs, and make-up, is sufficiently difficult. Add to these preparations constructing the Festival Theatre, literally from the ground up, and one marvels at Moiseiwitsch's stamina and leadership. The open stage had yet to be

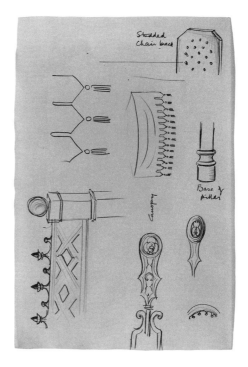

71. "Architectural Details and Designs," *Research Scrapbook* from *Richard III*, 1953, cat. no. 65

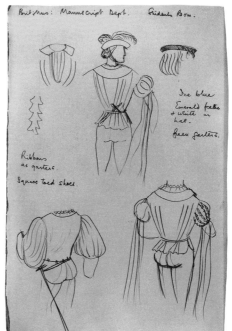

72. "Costume Studies," *Research Scrapbook* from *Richard III*, 1953, cat. no. 65

built—the site was still just a muddy hole in the ground—and a tent had to be sewn to house the auditorium. There was the complex challenge of finding the talent to execute the design plans in this small Canadian railway town of 19,000, tucked between Toronto and Detroit, whose sole theatrical asset was the coincidence of its name.

A theatrical designer relies on legions of individuals who share a vision and work together to bring it to life for opening night. In metropolitan London, long-reputed theater capital of the world, there is a concentrated wealth of theatrical know-how: scenic artists, stage carpenters, prop makers, wardrobe cutters, tailors, wig and hair stylists, jewelry makers, and milliners. Since there was no such talent pool to call upon in Stratford, Moiseiwitsch and Guthrie imported four trusted colleagues—Cecil Clarke as production manager, Ray Diffen as costume cutter, Annette Garceau as costumier, and Jacqueline Cundall to create stage properties. As they labored in temporary facilities, converted warehouses and borrowed halls, these dedicated professionals were pioneering a theater laboratory, planting and nurturing a Canadian production company practically overnight. Locating skilled craftspeople proved difficult, but not impossible. Clarke found a European immigrant shoemaker, for example, in a Toronto suburb about a hundred miles away; he executed Moiseiwitsch's plans in leather at his cobbler's bench in the Snug-fit Shoe Company, after providing several samples rendered from her designs.

In selecting an appropriate period in which to set the *Richard III* production, Guthrie and Moiseiwitsch had considered several factors. First, they wanted to strike a strong visual contrast with the other play of that inaugural season, *All's Well That Ends Well*, which would be performed in modern dress. The designer also sought to heighten the sense of Gothic terror in *Richard III*, and somehow treachery and horror seemed fitting to the late Dark Ages. "Historically, *Richard III* is more accurately placed at the end of the Middle Ages," explained Moiseiwitsch; although Richard ascended to the throne in 1483, "at Guthrie's behest, we decided to dress it earlier."[2] To give a frightening twist of the grotesque and to amplify the actors' stance and gesture in certain scenes, Moiseiwitsch slightly elongated the figures by exaggerating shapes, sleeve lengths, trains, and women's headpieces.

Of course, the primary goal was to use the costumes to help tell the story clearly. Guthrie and Moiseiwitsch understood that *Richard III*'s "complicated genealogy" and "rather obscure historical background, may have been a liability" for audiences, but they believed, along with Alec Guinness in the role of the king, that "the strong thread of melodrama would carry the day."[3] The text offered a built-in "who's who" by way of heraldic emblems, which the designer incorporated. The director alerted the audience to these in his program notes: "The War of the Roses was the name given to a protracted struggle between the House of Lancaster, whose emblem was the Red Rose, and that of York, whose emblem was the White.... In addition to the White Rose, the House of York was symbolized by A Sun." Guthrie also pointed out that Richard's personal emblem was a boar, and that this nickname was often used to refer to him in the play.[4] Guinness thus wore the image of a boar on a chain around his neck.

Dark, somber shades dominated the palette of the production, and Moiseiwitsch linked colors to emotions. She noted, for example, that "the murderers were in sad colors," and the awkward shape of one was rendered in "a sour color, not fashionable." Her rule of thumb in choosing hues was to give the impression that "t'was not a merry court." As she had in the past, Moiseiwitsch used color to highlight a moment or counterpoint an action within a scene. Noting the subtlety with which this was accomplished, audience member and author Robertson Davies cited an example: "The costumes for a large Shakespearean play must be designed so that the stage picture is effective at all times, with accents in the right places. This is not hard to manage when King Richard is on his throne, crowned and wearing his robe.... It is considerably more subtle when Richard, in his worn and dingy dress, is but one of a large group on the stage and his red (but not too red) cap is what keeps our eyes moving in his direction."[5]

73. *King Richard III, Scene 15* from *Richard III*, 1953, cat. no. 71

74. *Lady Anne* from *Richard III*, 1953, cat. no. 72 (photo: Collections of the Theatre Museum. By courtesy of the Board of Trustees of the Victoria and Albert Museum, London)

The massive robe that Guinness dragged behind him on the way to the throne in the coronation scene was blood red. In the play, explained Moiseiwitsch, "blood, a lot of blood, [was] spilt to get to that throne and so the whole stage was covered with red at that moment.... There was yardage—make that mileage—of red fabric." In the sketch depicting Richard's costume (fig. no. 73, color plate 25), with robe and crown trimmed in royal ermine, the designer brings to life the pomp and pageantry of the coronation, but also projects something of the macabre glee and physical deformity of this tragic figure. Empowered with the monarch's symbols, this Richard is not a hunchback, but there is a lump on

his left shoulder, created with layers of padding; his left eye is partially covered with a fold of skin, "so he physically looks crooked."[6]

Lady Anne first appears on stage in regal mourning, following the bier of her father-in-law, King Henry VI. But this rich black drapery cannot conceal her pale beauty. Interestingly, following the stylized design, actress Amelia Hall was instructed to substitute the normal ingenue's "peaches and cream" complexion when making up for a face as pale as possible, and with blue lips. For Lady Anne (fig. no. 74), Moiseiwitsch invented royal headgear—based on the double hennin cap with a wimple—by edging the cap

80

with a long golden crown. A wide belt, studded with light-catching metal diamond shapes, played against the deep black velvet of the voluminous gown and complemented the metallic ridge of the crown. Ermine trim accented the bodice, and long flowing sleeves heightened the figure's graceful curves.

Moiseiwitsch's sketch for Queen Margaret (fig. no. 75, color plate 27), showing an elongated tower hennin with a veil, and exaggerated sleeves, suggests a sinister, even supernatural quality perfectly suited to the widow of Henry VI, who hurls powerful prophecies and deadly curses. Thus costumed, Irene Worth truly inhabited the role. One enthusiastic reviewer wrote that "the actress creates a soaring picture of the witchlike, cursing Queen Margaret, whom bitterness has robbed of any concern for dignity."[7] Queen Elizabeth's and Queen Margaret's costumes were more colorful, within a limited palette, and fashionable for fashion's sake, than the somber apparel of Richard's mother, Dowager Duchess of York. The designs for all four female roles share a similarity of shape, silhouette, and accessory which immediately identifies them as royal and related. Moiseiwitsch visually strengthened these designs with a stylized theatrical translation of ermine, actually rendered in white flannel with long diagonal tails of black felt.

Contrite, with head covered in black, the sickly King Edward IV was a study in mortality and penitence, his life and color draining from his weakened frame. Moiseiwitsch wrapped him "in a white shiftlike shroud."[8] From references woven through the text, one surmises that Edward did not face death with ease. In the actual production, his cross pendant, pictured in Moiseiwitsch's costume sketch (fig. no. 76), was replaced by a gleaming gold chain with long links, possibly an allusion to Jane Shore, a London goldsmith's wife, who was Edward's mistress for many years. Perhaps this small cross became instead a giant processional crucifix, to create the powerful moment so exquisitely described by Davies:

75. *Queen Margaret* from *Richard III*, 1953, cat. no. 74

76. *King Edward IV, Sick* from *Richard III*, 1953, cat. no. 70

A procession of monks appeared from below the stage, bearing tapers and a huge Rood, upon which hung one of those figures of Christ, tortured and emaciated, in which the Gothic world took so much satisfaction. From the darkness at the back of the stage came Edward, not supported, but positively dragged, by two monks.... Painfully he was brought toward the Rood; with tenderness it was inclined toward him, and with a supreme effort the tortured King kissed the lips of the tortured God. Then, with new courage he set about his final task—the reconciliation of the factions of York and Lancaster. This was a great moment in the play, and a moment to live in memory.[9]

Reviewers agreed unanimously that both the designs and the stage were extraordinary. Brooks Atkinson, for the *New York Times*, wrote: "Miss Moiseiwitsch's costumes are bold and beautiful. The designs are powerful, the materials are rich; the contrast in color and shape is dramatic. When Mr. Guthrie sets the actors in motion, summoning state processionals from the pit, or setting opposing armies at each other's throats on the various stage levels, this is a *Richard III* that looks exciting." Lauretta Thistle of *Saturday Review* praised the "ample gorgeously colored costumes, the masterly handling of crowds, the magnificently staged processions, the larger-than-life shields,... crosses, and the stylized make-up." In the *New York Herald Tribune*, Walter Kerr stated that "Tanya Moiseiwitsch's architectural stage is brilliantly useful, her costumes almost invariably striking." Comparing *Richard III* and *All's Well That Ends Well*, he noted the plays' "radical contrasts in style," and likened the Richard production to exuberant illustrations for a Chaucer tale.[10]

The open stage on which these plays were performed has, since its initial use in 1953, been the object of much critical acclaim. Henry Hewes, for example, wrote that even "if the [Stratford] Festival had accomplished nothing else but the evolvement of Tanya Moiseiwitsch's functionally Elizabethan stage, it would have justified its existence. The formalized wooden setting of columns and steps provides a balcony and inner stage that lovers of Shakespeare on professional stages have often dreamed about, but seldom seen." Similarly, Atkinson pointed out that this stage "makes possible the fluidity and independence of scenery that Shakespearean drama thrives on." And C. Walter Hodges, eminent authority on the Shakespearean playhouse, summed it up succinctly, saying, "Tanya Moiseiwitsch is the designer of clearly the most successful modern translation of the original Elizabethan stage." The effectiveness of this modern stage has been proven over four decades at the Stratford Festival.[11]

The stage was actually a collaborative effort, a blend of Guthrie's knowledge as a director of Shakespeare and Moiseiwitsch's creative interpretation and design. For years they had grappled, independently and together, with the problems of Shakespearean production.[12] By the time they began to plan the Stratford, Ontario stage, Guthrie knew what he wanted and Moiseiwitsch knew how to combine the elements he thought essential. Working together at the Guthrie family home, Annagh-ma-Kerrig, near Monaghan, Ireland, in October 1952, they laid out their design. They agreed that "while conforming to the conventions of the Elizabethan theater in respect to practicalities, [the stage] should not present a pseudo-Elizabethan appearance." Guthrie stressed how determined they were "to eschew 'Ye Olde.'"[13] There would be no "olde" oak beams for the Festival Theatre, no rushes on the floor, nor ushers in Tudor costumes.

From their experience, they knew Shakespeare required "an upper level, a lower level, and a cellar," recalled Moiseiwitsch, explaining the origin of the design, "and that is what we were trying to conform to in simple terms—not elaborate. The more detail there is, the more it tends to 'pull' as the audience gets used to it." She remembered how they sought to keep the design "as bold as possible and let the actors and the props they bring on with them give the locality," a familiar practice for Moiseiwitsch by this

77. *Model of the Original Stage* from *Richard III*, 1953, cat. no. 66 (photo: Carlo Catenazzi)

time.[14] The resulting balsa wood model of the stage (fig. no. 77) Guthrie carefully balanced on his lap as he flew across the Atlantic in December that year.

In this innovative design for the Stratford stage, the upper level became an area of dominance so that an actor appearing in the apex of the balcony, framed by the opening behind him, commanded the stage. Rather than placing the balcony *within* the tiring house as John Crawford Adams had shown in his reconstructions of Shakespeare's Globe Playhouse,[15] Moiseiwitsch and Guthrie attached it to the front of the tiring house, without any rectangular frame that might have been construed as a small proscenium. This feature brought the action forward, giving it new dimension, reminiscent of Moiseiwitsch's treatment of the balcony and gallery for *Henry VIII* in 1949.

At the lower level, nine Tuscan pillars supported the balcony, and the position of the center pillar accentuated a ninety-degree angle. Later, without any word between the designer and the building architect, this pillar became the axis of the amphitheater seating. Although this pillar "isn't supporting the theater, it is in fact the very center of [what would become] the building, and for that reason," said Moiseiwitsch, "it is to me kind of a sacred pillar. It is in a firm position; actors gravitate towards it, and lean on it and swing around it." If instead two posts had been used on either side of the opening, a strong central entrance would have been created, leaving the side seats with poorer views. "We wanted to give the feeling that in the whole sweep—that one seat was as good as another," said Moiseiwitsch. "So on purpose, I blocked a center entrance."[16] By preventing direct downstage moves, the central pillar gave impetus to diagonal movement. It also stopped the eye from wandering beyond the central door frame on the lower level.

The nine pillars could suggest a "wooded place," "secluded area," or any other similar location required. Boxlike bases could be added to the columns for seating. The cellar level, used for graves or entrances to dungeons, was created by cutting a trap

78

79

80

81

82

78. *Alderman* from *Richard III*, 1953, cat. no. 67

79. *Cardinal Bourchier, Scene 7* from *Richard III*, 1953, cat. no. 68

80. *Guards and Men at Arms* from *Richard III*, 1953, cat. no. 69

81. *Lord Mayor, Scenes 7, 11, and 13* from *Richard III*, 1953, cat. no. 73

82. *Sir Richard Ratcliff* from *Richard III*, 1953, cat. no. 75

door into the floor on the platform. The moat, a sunken area surrounding the stage, was designed to keep the actors' heads and bodies from obstructing sight lines when they were required to be on the edges of the action.

The architectural setting offered "standing places, seats, and things to lean against.... Everything had a practical purpose and was not there just to look pretty," Moiseiwitsch explained. One important feature of the design was that it was solid structurally. "Solidity to me," Moiseiwitsch continued, "is a great joy. Actors can throw themselves against the pillars, fling themselves down the stairs, and there's no wobble.... To me all the illusion that they're trying to create goes when the floor gives way.... I find that very bothering."[17] Sticking doors and shaking walls, problems of traditional stock scenery, were eliminated by creating a sturdy setting, a place "planned by Dr. Guthrie and me," said Moiseiwitsch, "as a place to *act*—uncluttered and yet fairly intimate."[18]

Because it located audience and actor in the same room, Moiseiwitsch's open stage had a powerful impact on the design of costumes and properties. With the audience gathered around the stage, the two-dimensional illusions for creating proscenium stage pictures became outmoded: painted flats, wings and borders, footlights, all the scenic investiture that depended on viewing the stage picture from a single point was rendered useless. Moiseiwitsch found that designing for the open stage was more like molding a sculpture than painting a canvas. Greater emphasis had to be placed on the shape and texture of the costumes, now viewed from all sides: the nap of the cloth, the drape and cut of the clothes had to be most expressive. To enhance the depth of draped or gathered material, folds were skillfully shaded with dyes. Often newly made costumes were "broken down" by carefully fraying, creasing, daubing with paint, or scraping with a kitchen grater to look as though they had been worn for years.

With the entire audience seated within sixty-five feet of the stage, stitching on garments had to look hand-sewn; hooks and bars were the only fasteners acceptable, since the suggestion of an historical period could be spoiled by the glimpse of a modern zipper. Footwear, too, became more prominent on the open stage. Running from a tunnel or descending the three steps surrounding the acting platform, actors' feet were suddenly more visible and consequently demanded the designer's special attention. Even the material used for heels and soles was a consideration in producing the footfall appropriate to the character. Soles were halved with leather for sound and rubber for traction, and the entire sole of the shoe was dyed black so as not to appear new.

The Stratford experiment showed the designer and director more strengths than weaknesses during the first seasons, and ultimately revolutionized the mounting of Shakespeare's plays. Clarke, production manager in the first year, wondered whether this stage would "achieve universal popularity and become, as it were, the blueprint for Shakespearean and perhaps other classical productions in the years to come...."[19] Soon after, drama critic Kerr noted, "On this stage designed by Tanya Moiseiwitsch we find...the actors working out in the open in a tremendously plastic and sculptured manner...," and "[we] come directly back into touch with the tremendous intimacy, with the aliveness, with the kind of electric quality that the plays have when...they are left alone right out in the open.... I believe that this theater," Kerr concluded, "is setting a standard for physical production, for Shakespearean style, for verse speech, that the rest of this continent can well emulate, and for which it must be very, very deeply grateful."[20]

The Stratford stage did in fact become a prototype for the open stages Moiseiwitsch would design for the Guthrie Theater in Minneapolis and the Crucible Theatre in Sheffield, England. In addition, this open stage would inspire the construction of many others—Lincoln Center's Vivian Beaumont; the Festival Theatre, Chicester, England; the National Arts Center, Ottawa; the Mark Taper Forum, Los Angeles; the South Australia Theatre Company, Adelaide Festival Centre; and numerous theaters located at major universities such as the Court Theatre at the University of Chicago and the Stoll Theater at the University of Minnesota, to name but two. Moiseiwitsch's accomplishments at Stratford, Ontario would also lead to her appointment to the Building Committee for the National Theatre of Great Britain. G. Wilson Knight referred to Stratford as the "'headquarters' today of open stage Shake-spearean presentation," and stated that it "has become a model, since followed in England and the United States, of theatrical design...the culmination of the drive for Elizabethan simplicity and freedom...."[21]

NOTES

1. Robertson Davies in Davies, Tyrone Guthrie, and Grant MacDon-ald, *Renown at Stratford*, 2d ed. (1953; reprint, Toronto: Clarke, Irwin and Co., 1971), 43.

2. Tanya Moiseiwitsch, interview with the author, Stratford, Ontario, 24 June 1992, hereafter cited as "author interview."

3. Davies in Davies et al., *Renown at Stratford*, 9.

4. "Notes on 'Richard III,'" in "The Tragedy of King Richard III, 1953," Program of the Stratford Shakespearean Festival of Canada Foundation, n.p.

5. Davies in Davies et al., *Renown at Stratford*, 99.

6. Author interview.

7. Lauretta Thistle, review of *Richard III* and *All's Well That Ends Well*, *Saturday Review of Literature*, July 1953, n.p. Press Clipping Book, Stratford Festival Archives, Ontario.

8. Davies in Davies et al., *Renown at Stratford*, 87.

9. Ibid.

10. Brooks Atkinson, "At the Theatre," *The New York Times*, 14 July 1953; Thistle, review of *Richard III*; Walter Kerr, "Festival Surprise: 'All's Well's a Hit," *New York Herald Tribune*, 18 July 1953.

11. Henry Hewes, "Astringency in Ontario," *Saturday Review of Literature*, 4 June 1955, 26; Brooks Atkinson, "Canada's Stratford Shakespeare Festival Off to Good Start," *New York Times*, 19 July 1953; C. Walter Hodges interviewed by the author, Kent, Ohio, 5 November 1979.

12. See Tyrone Guthrie, *A Life in the Theatre* (New York: McGraw-Hill, 1959), 121, 190–92, and 307–13. Guthrie describes two experiences that directly influenced his ideas about the design of the open stage: the emergency staging of *Hamlet* in the round at Elsinore and the 1948 pro-duction of *The Three Estates* on a contrived platform stage with seating on three sides in the Assembly Hall in Edinburgh, Scotland.

13. Guthrie in Davies et al., *Renown at Stratford*, 8.

14. Moiseiwitsch, interviewed by Karl T. Pope in "Historical Study of the Stratford Ontario Festival Theatre," Ph.D. diss., Wayne State Univer-sity, 1965, 56, hereafter cited as "Pope interview."

15. John Crawford Adams, *The Globe Playhouse: Its Design and Equipment*, 1st ed. (Cambridge, Mass.: Harvard University Press, 1942). "Tiring house" is an Elizabethan term refering to the space immediately behind the stage where actors "retired" once they exited a scene. It was often the location of the dressing rooms and prop/costume storage.

16. Pope interview, 58.

17. Ibid., 60.

18. Moiseiwitsch, interviewed by Thom Benson, C.B.C. documentary, 26 June 1962, C.B.C. Radio Archives, Toronto.

19. Cecil Clarke, Stratford Shakespeare Festival Souvenir Program, 1953, Stratford Festival Archives.

20. Walter Kerr, International Service Address, 29 July 1954. Press-book no. 9, 1953–1957, Stratford Festival Archives.

21. G. Wilson Knight, *Shakespearean Production with Special Refer-ence to the Tragedies* (Evanston, Ill.: Northwestern University Press, 1964), 291.

RICHARD III

Stratford Festival Theatre
Ontario, 1953
Directed by Tyrone Guthrie

65
Research Scrapbook
Pencil on paper, each 14 1/2 x 9 5/8
(36.8 x 24.3)
The Stratford Festival, Canada

66
Model of the Original Stage
Balsa wood, 12 x 16 3/4 x 24 1/4
(30.5 x 42.5 x 61.6)
The Stratford Festival, Canada

67
Alderman (Vincent Edward)
Pencil, pen and ink, watercolor on paper,
15 5/8 x 11 3/8 (39.7 x 28.9)
The Stratford Festival, Canada

68
Cardinal Bourchier, Scene 7 (Peter Mews)
Pencil, watercolor on paper, 14 1/4 x 8
(36.2 x 20.3), image
Courtesy of Mrs. A. M. Bell

69
Guards and Men at Arms
Pencil, gouache, brush and ink, watercolor on
paper, 17 7/8 x 11 3/16 (45.4 x 28.4)
Tanya Moiseiwitsch Collection

70
King Edward IV, Sick (Edward Holmes)
Pencil, brush and ink, watercolor on paper,
15 15/16 x 11 7/16 (40.5 x 29.1)
Tanya Moiseiwitsch Collection

71
King Richard III, Scene 15 (Alec Guinness)
Pencil, watercolor, pen and ink, body color on
paper, 15 1/8 x 13 1/2 (38.4 x 34.3)
The Stratford Festival, Canada

72
Lady Anne (Amelia Hall)
Pencil, watercolor on paper, 17 7/8 x 12 1/8
(38 x 30.5), image
From the Collections of the Theatre Museum.
By courtesy of the Board of Trustees of the
Victoria and Albert Museum, London

73
Lord Mayor, Scenes 7, 11, and 13
(Michael Bates)
Pencil, pen and ink, gouache on paper,
15 1/4 x 11 (38.7 x 28)
The Stratford Festival, Canada

74
Queen Margaret (Irene Worth)
Pencil, gouache, pen and ink, watercolor on
paper, 16 1/4 x 12 15/16 (41.3 x 32.9)
The Stratford Festival, Canada

75
Sir Richard Ratcliff (Robert Robinson)
Pencil, brush and ink, watercolor on paper,
15 15/16 x 11 1/4 (40.5 x 28.6)
Tanya Moiseiwitsch Collection

76*
Coronation Robes
Red velvet with ermine trim, 216 (547.8)
The Stratford Festival, Canada

Alec Guinness as King Richard in *Richard III*,
Stratford Festival, Ontario, 1953 (photo: Peter Smith.
The Stratford Festival, Canada)

But all along, the thing that frightened me most was that the theater wouldn't be ready in time, the props certainly couldn't possibly be ready and the armor wouldn't have even dried and the weather was very hot and there were awful thunderstorms. None of that was true—I mean, the thunderstorms were true but everything was ready, everything happened on the first night of Richard III, July 13, 1953. By the time Alec Guiness got to the throne, the whole of the stage was covered in the forty yards of his red velvet cloak. And that wasn't just showing-off-costume time. That was Guthrie. The thought behind it was to get to the throne he had killed a lot of people and this was an ocean of blood that he was carrying as a burden on his shoulders. Did everybody know what they were meant to think? No, absolutely not. But that was the thought behind it.

Also adapted from an interview by Therese Greenwood, 25 July 1992, *The Whig-Standard Magazine*

Irene Worth as Queen Margaret in *Richard III* at the
Stratford Festival, Ontario, 1953 (photo: Peter Smith.
The Stratford Festival, Canada)

The Winter's Tale

Stratford Festival Theatre
Ontario, 1958

IN THE LAST ACT of *The Winter's Tale*, King Leontes, surrounded by his somber Sicilian court, eagerly awaits his lost daughter, Perdita, who had been abandoned as a baby some sixteen years earlier. As she bursts into the gathering, accompanied by her lover, Florizel, the old king exclaims, "Welcome hither, as is spring to the earth." Describing this moment in the 1958 Stratford Festival production designed by Tanya Moiseiwitsch, one theater-goer reported how "color...reaches a climax all its own in the scene," and noticed that the impact of the young couple's entrance was precisely like the arrival of spring: "Florizel and Perdita are [dressed] in gay, bright greens and pinks; Leontes and his court...in blacks, grays, brown and scarlet."[1] Here was a visual metaphor of the play created through color and movement, as if the newly sprouted promises of spring blossomed, pushing aside dead leaves blackened by last winter's storms. This was but one example of the artistry of the designer and the staging skills of her longtime friend Douglas Campbell, making his directing debut with this production of *The Winter's Tale*. The director had assembled a distinguished cast, featuring Christopher Plummer, Eileen Herlie, Frances Hyland, and Jason Robards, Jr. An actor himself, Campbell had been a member of the Stratford Festival from its inception, earning critical acclaim for his remarkable talents. Now during his sixth season, besides portraying Falstaff in *Henry IV, Part I*, he was exploring his talent in directing. Over the years, a deep friendship and respect had grown between him and Moiseiwitsch; with this project their professional relationship would develop anew.

Both director and designer were new to the script, and together they sifted through *The Winter's Tale*, searching for a possible approach. Eventually they identified the difficulties presented by the text. First and most obvious was the plot's huge leap in time—sixteen years slide by between acts 3 and 4. Shakespeare,

reworking Robert Greene's story *Pandosta, The Triumph of Time* (1588), had introduced a narrator to span this chasm in the chronology. The collaborators now cast this character as Father Time, who would carry a huge hour glass. The play, peppered with allusions, conjures various historical periods, particularly classical Greece, and has the flavor of a fantasy or fable. The story also delineates a contrast between two worlds: the Sicilian court of Leontes, with its despair and confusion, and the robust country life, born of simplicity and nature. The production design, whatever it was to be, needed to express this fundamental difference.

For Campbell, the glowing canvases of the seventeenth-century Flemish painter Peter Paul Rubens struck a chord, especially for their use of myths, allegories, and classical themes. "There was also something about Rubens' fat, naked ladies lying about the fields that seemed very much like [the bucolic sensuality of the shepherd scenes] we were trying to achieve," chuckled Moiseiwitsch.[2] Rubens became their reference point for color and silhouette, and for the classical appearance of the court. But Campbell also wished to show Leontes' court "as a place of disease and despair, with the King's jealousy of his Queen, Hermione, as the climaxing sickness."[3] To express the court's decadence, the director devised an introduction to the first scene, a kind of visual and mythological preface to the play.

For this introductory moment, Ken LeMaire took the role of Bacchus, with Tammy Grimes, Anna Reiser, and Joyce Kirkpatrick as bacchantes. Donald Ewer played Perseus, Eric Christmas, a satyr, Ann Morrish portrayed Andromache, and James Peddie, Eros. "A Bacchanalian masque took place off stage, so it was never actually seen by the audience," explained Moiseiwitsch.[4] When the merry troupe, well into their cups, returned to the stage, the cart belonging to Bacchus had been taken over by Plummer as Leontes, and the play's first scene commenced. This staging device served a dual purpose, cleverly introducing the Greco-Roman mythological world and providing, at least for a time, probable cause for Leontes' otherwise irrational behavior: the king's unfounded accusations of an illicit relationship between

83. *Time* from *The Winter's Tale*, 1958, cat. no. 90

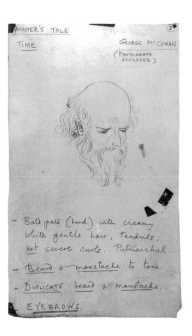

84. *Wig Sketch for Time* from *The Winter's Tale*, 1958, cat. no. 91

his wife and his visiting friend Polixenes could be attributed to drink.

It is fascinating to explore Campbell's interpretation of Shakespeare's text and to trace his designer's visualizations of character and theme. Moiseiwitsch's painted renderings for *The Winter's Tale* show a departure from her normal working method. Usually, research notes and pencil sketches crammed her notebooks in preparation for the watercolors she reserved for the later stages of a design's evolution. In this case, however, Moiseiwitsch chose a new medium. At the suggestion of actor James Mason, who was also a painter, Moiseiwitsch began experimenting with casein on canvas, on a larger scale than ever before. Working in this new medium and scale, she found great release. Rather than rendering just one figure in a drawing, she found herself painting several, in fact, the whole masque scene which was planned to begin the play. In casein, pigment is mixed with water and milk to provide a vehicle and binder for the color; the opaque quality that results may be a possible explanation for the rich and deeply saturated color that became this *Winter's Tale* palette: shades of blue, copper, orange, purple, black, and gray (of autumn and winter) for the court; with lighter tints of green, cream, pink, and yellow (of spring) for the country. All this is reflected in the costume bible (fig. no. 85).

The costume or wardrobe department, following common theater practice, holds all notes, instructions, fabric swatches, and cast measurements, and even copies of the designer's renderings or working drawings in an organized and portable notebook for each production. Sometimes compiled by the designer or supervisor in charge of a workroom, the costume bible gives a complete inventory of each character's costumes, wigs, hats, accessories, and costume changes required, and provides the researcher a fairly accurate picture of the materials used to fabricate the costume. From these pages, one learns that in *The Winter's Tale* Leontes appeared in the first scene in a Romanesque cuirass of velveteen with detailed fabric painting and appliqué (fig. no. 86). With a laurel wreath, rather than a kingly crown, the designer suggests the clas-

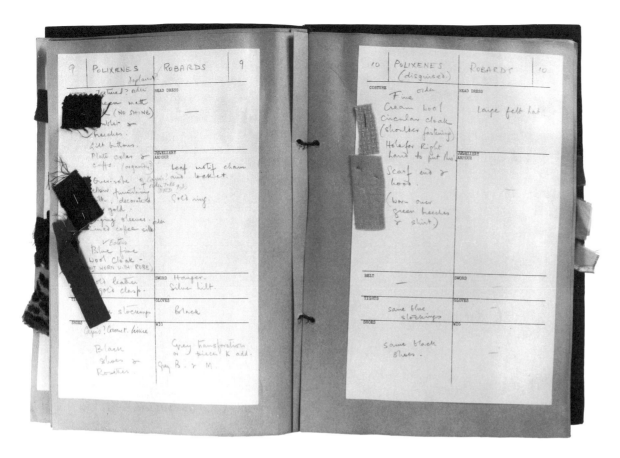

85. "Costume for Polixenes," *Costume Bible* from *The Winter's Tale*, 1958, cat. no. 78

sical period, and the scarlet silk lining, with slashed sleeves showing a white shirt, is contrasted with the royal purple velvet drape. The tawny gold of the cuirass may have been inspired by Leontes' namesake, the king of the jungle.

Queen Hermione, played by Charmion King, was dressed in tangerine-shot taffeta with sleeves appliquéd in gold, pearls, and studs. White marquisette was used at the neck and through the sleeves; a pale pink and yellow-shot organza drape completed the costume. The queen wore a tiara, and pearls and beads were intertwined in her hair. Other accessories included a necklace which hooked to the bodice, shoulder brooches, rings, and golden slippers. Padding indicated her pregnancy. For the scene when she is plucked from her palace chambers and taken off to prison, Hermione wore a blue velveteen robe trimmed with brown fur,

and a light blue underrobe (fig. no. 88, color plate 30). A duplicate of this underrobe was created, then aged, stained with dyes, and distressed to indicate time's passage for the following scene, the trial. For this scene, the pregnant padding was deleted, as Hermione's child had been born in prison. From her shoulders draped a length of mushroom-colored nylon tricot, and from her hair hung a veil of pale gray silk jersey, as she was led to judgment.

Paulina, wife of the courtier Antigonus and the queen's loyal friend, was played by Herlie. Like Hermione, she was dressed in blue, but a deeper, richer shade, her gown trimmed in brown fur, with a copper-colored underskirt (fig. no. 89). Paulina wore gold beads, pearl necklaces, and pearls in her hair. Clearly, the designer meant to team these two characters, linking them with similar

86

87

88

89

86. *Leontes* from *The Winter's Tale*, 1958, cat. no. 84

87. *Autolicus* from *The Winter's Tale*, 1958, cat. no. 79

88. *Hermione, Act 3* from *The Winter's Tale*, 1958, cat. no. 83

89. *Paulina* from *The Winter's Tale*, 1958, cat. no. 87

shapes and color of clothing and accessories. Designs for the courtier Camillo (fig. nos. 90, 91, color plate 29), acted by Powys Thomas, combined the silhouette of the 1600s—high collar, black doublet, hose, and knee breeches—with light-copper classical drapery, attached at the shoulders and carried togalike over the arm. As in all the rich design for the court, there is the feeling of weight and volume to these clothes, befitting their formality and rank, as well as forming a striking contrast with the world of the country shepherds in the spring.

This contrast is most dramatically apparent in the costume for Perdita, the lost child, now sixteen years of age, enacted by Hyland. Her flowing gown was a diaphanous pink chiffon, trimmed with leaves and painted flowers, with a yellow undergarment; her head was crowned with a wreath of flowers, and she was fitted with sandals. Botticelli-like, she personified spring. Florizel, played by Peter Donat, was disguised as Doricles, and consistent with the rustic style, was garbed in a no-shine silk jacket with light blue trim, breeches, poplin shirt, a belt of natural leather, and cream-colored fine wool cloak. With a large straw hat to shade his eyes in the bright meadow's sunshine, he carried a shepherd's crook with a bow. The Old Shepherd, played by Mervyn Blake, was costumed in sheepskin, straw hat, thick corduroy breeches with a blue hanky, and a full beard that was noted to be "curly and sheeplike."

A sketch for hats for the three judges (fig. no. 92) gives evidence of the designer's concern for detail. Built for each individual actor, the respective hats must nevertheless match in style and proportion. Moiseiwitsch's notes clarify the particulars of construction, and indicate where ties should be placed so as not to obstruct the actor's face. The sketch for a shepherd's hat for Robards's Polixenes (fig. no. 93) defines the shape and the material to be used, identifies the stock wig to be worn, and notes that the hood of the cloak will be prepared in wardrobe, rather than the millinery shop. Dirk Campbell, in the role of Mamillius, Leontes' son, was to wear a beret of blue taffeta (fig. no. 94), most probably of the same fabric used to fashion his costume (fig. no. 95).

90. *Camillo, A Lord of Sicilia, Act 1* from *The Winter's Tale*, 1958, cat. no. 80

91. *Camillo, Act 2* from *The Winter's Tale*, 1958, cat. no. 81

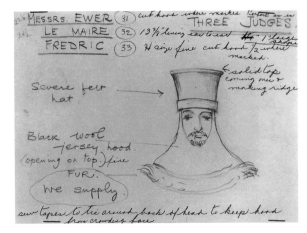

92

93

94

95

92. *Headwear Sketch for the Three Judges* from *The Winter's Tale*, 1958, cat. no. 89

93. *Headwear Sketch for Polixenes* from *The Winter's Tale*, 1958, cat. no. 88

94. *Headwear Sketch for Mamillius* from *The Winter's Tale*, 1958, cat. no. 86

95. *Mamillius* from *The Winter's Tale*, 1958, cat. no. 85

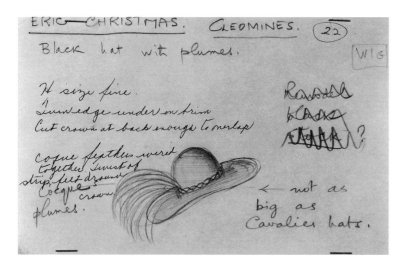

ERIC CHRISTMAS. CLEOMINES. (22)

Black hat with plumes.

WIG

H size fine.
Turn edge under on trim
Cut crown at back enough to overlap

Coque feathers wired
together. Twist of
strip, felt around
Coque crown
plumes.

Random
black
plumes ?

← not as
big as
Cavalier hats.

96. *Headwear Sketch for Cleomines* from *The Winter's Tale*, 1958,
cat. no. 82

The pale pink and coffee-colored plumes had to be in proportion to the width of Mamillius's hat. How big should the hat be? The ten-year-old actor's head measured 20 1/2 inches, but there is a reminder on the sketch to add a bit more room because he would be wearing a wig.

One can sometimes look at Moiseiwitsch's renderings for these costumes and see only a sketch or painting, forgetting that they constitute a guide for a wardrobe department—cutters, stitchers, finishers, and drapers—to help realize a vision, an actor creating a character for a moment on stage. Costumes must withstand the rigors of an entire summer season of performances, with repeated cleanings and pressings. And they must fit so as not to restrict the actor from any action required by the director, be it plunging a sword, falling to the ground, or climbing to a balcony. Examining Moiseiwitsch's plans and notations made for the craftspersons executing the designs, one gets a glimpse of how the drawings would be transformed into durable attire. All these are *working* drawings, meant to be highly expressive and communicative, guiding skilled hands backstage. They are records of the back-and-forth of true artistic collaboration required in any theatrical production.

The critical reception of *The Winter's Tale* was mixed, with varied responses to the design, direction, acting, and the text. Brooks Atkinson wrote for the *New York Times* that the open-stage production stressed "spectacular processionals with flambeaux, big court scenes with many attendants and minor ceremonies, off-stage tumult, stunning costumes, ornate properties. The opening scene...has the weight and impact of one of the tragedies." Yet this same reviewer also believed the play could not "support the drive and conviction of the bravura scenes," because it is a fable, an entertainment that "thrives better on the lighter style." Generally praising the acting, especially in the comic pastoral scenes, he commented that with all the emphasis "on movement, spectacle, and regal splendor,...the innocent play of *The Winter's Tale* is almost an after thought." John Beaufort, for the *Christian Science Monitor*, reported *The Winter's Tale* was one of Moiseiwitsch's most elaborate productions. Though he praised her for "providing a splendidly classically mythical spectacle," he found the rich appointments in the opening scene distracting. Herbert Whittaker of the *Toronto Globe and Mail* noted, "The Festival has once again matched its own high standards. There is so much of what the dramatist has termed 'a notable passion of wonder' to be found here that it is as if one has lived a whole life of theater in the hours of its performing."[5]

The standards Whittaker praised were, of course, those to which Moiseiwitsch herself always adhered. By 1958, she had more than two decades experience as a professional designer, and her work had been seen, with frequency, on both sides of the Atlantic. Her design credits for this one year alone attest to her outstanding reputation as a much-sought-after talent. In addition to *The Winter's Tale*, she designed, with Marie Day, the Stratford Festival's *Henry IV, Part I*. For Stratford-upon-Avon's Shakespeare Memorial Theatre, she created the sets for *Much Ado about Nothing*. That same year, London West End audiences applauded her contemporary designs for J. M. Fulton's *The Bright One*, at the Winter Garden Theatre. Then, turning her attention again to Canada, she designed the Stratford Festival's Canadian tour of *Two Gentlemen of Verona*, and an adaptation of Heinrich von Kleist's *The Broken Jug*, which subsequently played a limited Broadway engagement at the Phoenix Theatre. During the two previous seasons, her designs for the stage had been seen at Scotland's prestigious Edinburgh Festival, London's Old Vic, Strat-ford-upon-Avon, and Broadway's Royal Theatre with productions of *Oedipus Rex*, *Two Gentlemen of Verona*, *Measure for Measure*, and Thornton Wilder's *Matchmaker*, respectively. Moiseiwitsch's drive, versatility, and design contributions proved as astonishing as her consistently high ideals of artistic achievement.

NOTES

1. Alan Haydock, "3rd Festival Play Busy Production," *The Stratford Beacon Herald*, 22 July 1958.

2. Tanya Moiseiwitsch, interview with the author, Stratford, Ontario, 24 June 1992, hereafter cited as "author interview."

3. Herbert Whittaker, "A Vivid Telling of 'Winter's Tale,'" *The Globe Magazine*, July 1958, 3.

4. Author interview.

5. Brooks Atkinson, "Two 'Winter's Tales'—Avon and Housatonic," *New York Times*, reprinted in *The Montreal Star*, 26 July 1958; John Beaufort, "Twice-told 'Winter's Tale'—Shakespeare at Stratford in Ontario and Connecticut," *The Christian Science Monitor*, 26 July 1958; Herbert Whittaker, quoted by Ron Evans, "Spectacular 'Winter's Tale' Given Stratford Premiere," *The Evening Times Globe*, 22 July 1958. *Winter's Tale* Press Clipping Book, Stratford Festival Archives, Ontario.

THE WINTER'S TALE

The Stratford Festival Theatre
Ontario, 1958
Directed by Douglas Campbell

77*
Costume Bible
Pencil, fabric swatches on paper, 16 1/8 x
11 1/2 x 1 1/4 (41 x 29.2 x 3.3), closed
The Stratford Festival, Canada

78
Costume Bible
Pencil, fabric swatches on paper, 16 1/4 x
11 7/8 x 3/4 (41.3 x 30.2 x 1.9), closed
The Stratford Festival, Canada

79
Autolicus (Bruno Gerussi)
Pencil, casein on linen paper,
13 7/8 x 9 15/16 (34.6 x 25.2)
Tanya Moiseiwitsch Collection

80
Camillo, A Lord of Sicilia, Act 1
(Powys Thomas)
Pencil, casein on linen paper,
14 1/4 x 10 7/16 (36.2 x 26.5)
Tanya Moiseiwitsch Collection

81
Camillo, Act 2
Casein, pencil, brush and ink on linen paper,
13 3/4 x 9 1/2 (35 x 24)
The Stratford Festival, Canada

82
Headwear Sketch for Cleomines
(Eric Christmas)
Pencil, red pencil, ballpoint pen on paper,
5 9/16 x 8 9/16 (14.2 x 21.8)
The Stratford Festival, Canada

83
Hermione, Act 3 (Charmion King)
Casein, pencil, pen and ink on linen paper,
13 7/8 x 10 1/2 (35.2 x 26.6)
The Stratford Festival, Canada

84
Leontes (Christopher Plummer)
Pencil, casein on linen paper,
13 1/2 x 9 15/16 (34.3 x 24), image
Gallery/Stratford, Stratford, Ontario,
gift of Mr. Floyd Chalmers

85
Mamillius (Dirk Campbell)
Pencil, casein on linen paper,
12 3/8 x 8 7/8 (31.4 x 22.1)
Courtesy of Dirk Campbell

86
Headwear Sketch for Mamillius
Pencil, ballpoint pen, fabric swatch on paper,
7 7/16 x 8 9/16 (18.9 x 21.7)
The Stratford Festival, Canada

87
Paulina (Eileen Herlie)
Pencil, casein on linen paper, 13 15/16 x
9 15/16 (35.4 x 25.3), image
Gallery/Stratford, Stratford, Ontario,
gift of Mr. Floyd Chalmers

88
Headwear Sketch for Polixenes
(Jason Robards, Jr.)
Pencil, red pencil, ballpoint pen on paper,
6 1/2 x 8 1/2 (16.4 x 21.7)
The Stratford Festival, Canada

89
Headwear Sketch for the Three Judges
(Messrs. Ewer, LeMaire, Frederic)
Pencil, ballpoint pen on paper, 6 1/4 x 8 3/8
(16 x 21.7)
The Stratford Festival, Canada

90
Time (George McCowan)
Pencil, casein on linen paper,
14 11/16 x 10 1/2 (37.3 x 26.7)
Tanya Moiseiwitsch Collection

91
Wig Sketch for Time
Pencil on paper, 13 7/8 x 8 1/2 (35.3 x 21.6)
The Stratford Festival, Canada

92*
Tunic for Leontes
Velvet, silk, felt, braid, cast plastic, 35 (89)
The Stratford Festival, Canada

Opposite: Jason Robards, Jr. as
Polixenes, Powys Thomas as Camillo,
Charmion King as Hermione, and
Christopher Plummer as Leontes in
The Winter's Tale, Stratford Festival,
Ontario, 1958 (photo: Herb Nott.
The Stratford Festival, Canada)

Frances Hyland as Perdita in *The
Winter's Tale*, Stratford Festival,
Ontario, 1958 (photo: Herb Nott.
The Stratford Festival, Canada)

Overleaf: Eileen Herlie as Paulina,
Charmion King as Hermione, and
Sydney Sturgess and Deborah Turnbull
as Ladies-in-Waiting in *The Winter's
Tale*, Stratford Festival, Ontario, 1958
(photo: Herb Nott. The Stratford
Festival, Canada)

The House of Atreus

Guthrie Theater
Minneapolis, 1967

WHEN THE GUTHRIE THEATER opened *The House of Atreus* on 21 July 1967, it was, according to Tyrone Guthrie's biographer James Forsyth, "quite a moment in Life and in Art." Forsyth stated that "if the whole achievement of Stratford, Ontario, was the crown of Guthrie's career, this production was the peak of his artistic achievement." The same could be said for his designer, Tanya Moiseiwitsch. "Awesome and timeless," were the words *Newsweek* used to describe her design, while another reviewer praised it as her "finest hour." The *New York Times* called the work superb, and declared that Guthrie and Moiseiwitsch had "accomplished what has never been done before on this continent, and seldom anywhere else outside Greece…. They have made an artistic, popular and even an historical success out of the *Oresteia* of Aeschylus, which they choose to call *The House of Atreus*…draw[ing] a moving, elevating, even harrowing experience."[1] The production would become legendary in theatrical circles.

Although the press release for the Guthrie's staging of the monumental trilogy proclaimed that the work had been three years in the making, the production in fact drew on two lifetimes of work in the theater. For the director, this was a reflection, if not a validation, of his theory of drama as ritual, and for Moiseiwitsch, it was a stunning culmination of her theatrical expertise and artistry for the open stage. She had served as principal designer of the Guthrie Theater from its opening in 1963 through 1966. Building on her achievement at Stratford with the successful open stage for Shakespeare, Moiseiwitsch created in Minneapolis a flexible environment, with an asymmetrical open stage for classical drama, both ancient and modern. She also played a critical role in planning the backstage, wardrobe, costume, and production areas. Once opened, the Guthrie helped to usher in a new chapter in America's artistic and cultural growth, as the flagship of the resident theater movement. *The House of Atreus* did much to illumine the young theater's shining reputation.

Moiseiwitsch's design ideas for a masked production of this classical Greek trilogy can be traced to several seminal experiences. Perhaps foremost was designing *Oedipus Rex* in 1954 for the Stratford Festival's stage, which shares some similarity with a Greek amphitheater, its audience nearly surrounding the players. Her designs for the production, which starred James Mason in the title role, capitalized boldly on three-dimensional shapes and enlarged human proportions. Moreover, Moiseiwitsch came to believe, as did Guthrie, that drama is a kind of ritual, not unlike a religious rite. An audience, like a congregation, gathers to participate in a symbolic or stylized act. They accept the action on stage not because it is real, but because they allow themselves to become imaginatively involved. Guthrie's ritual theory, derived from the actual role of drama in ancient Greece, influenced Moiseiwitsch's approach to *Oedipus Rex*; her designs encouraged the audience to receive the play symbolically rather than realistically.[2]

To achieve this, the personalities of the actors in *Oedipus Rex* were minimized by covering faces, limbs, and hands to show the least possible human individuality. Guthrie and Moiseiwitsch believed that Greek actors had worn masks so that "no detail of personality [could] intervene between the audience and the tragic symbol." By concealing his or her face "behind the impersonal, but not unexpressive features of a mask," the actor could become anonymous, a mere channel for something greater. In addition, to make the legendary tragic heroes or "great ones" literally greater, the use of the cothurnus, the elevated Greek boot, seemed absolutely necessary. By heightening shoe soles four to six inches and designing masks one and a half times life size, the designer and director sought to "create the…effect of rather strange greatness and impressiveness."[3] Moiseiwitsch's plan combined the mask and costume to enlarge and dignify the wearer, who participated in a story that was larger than life.

This ritual design became a means of communicating a world of magnitude more powerful than the realistic stage; the production, later revived and filmed, was to become a definitive performance popularizing *Oedipus Rex* for many, and survives as a permanent record of Moiseiwitsch's stunning talent. The designer, moreover, took from this production several important lessons for *The House of Atreus*, in which the same style of stagecraft and theory of drama were brought forward and amplified thirteen years later. She had seen that Guthrie's concept of ritual theater, particularly the notion of symbolic re-enactment, could be effectively implemented with masks and cothurni. Methods for crafting these designs had been determined, though it was clear that the artisans needed more time to execute properties, costumes, and masks. Moiseiwitsch also knew that some form of masks and cothurni proved necessary during early rehearsals to acquaint the actors with the challenge of moving while in costume.

Comparing *Oedipus Rex* and *The House of Atreus*, Moiseiwitsch pointed out that the latter was much more challenging, since it condensed three full-length tragedies into one evening: "It was three times larger, took not only three times as long to prepare, but really, it seemed like a lifetime of preparation."[4] Planning for the designs began more than a year before the production opened, and they were much bolder, less intricate in detail than those for *Oedipus Rex*. The drawings themselves are larger, and Moiseiwitsch appears to have acquired more freedom, more willingness to abstract lines, shapes, and volumes. Although masks were again used to achieve a more universal statement, it is important to understand that Moiseiwitsch and Guthrie were *not* seeking some historical reconstruction of classical Greek staging practices. The director explained that they incorporated "devices the Greek theater is known to have used—not only choral speech, but impersonal masks and so on," but he added that their intention was not "to reconstruct the sort of impressions which an Athenian audience may have felt twenty-five hundred years ago."[5] Instead, their aim was to recreate archetypal situations in a vivid theatrical

event. And they succeeded. "It is the only revival of a Greek tragedy that I have ever seen; all the others were mere exhumations," stated one drama critic.[6] Guthrie regarded Aeschylus's trilogy (458 B.C.) not only as "the foundation stone of the art of drama," but also as "one of the greatest expressions which the human spirit has ever achieved." In these three plays, *Agamemnon*, *The Bringers of Offerings*, and *The Furies*, a justice "wiser and more sophisticated than the primitive order of [an] eye for an eye" emerges.[7] *The House of Atreus* is concerned with the emerging concept of a god who transcends the vengeful tribal deity represented by the Furies, for a god as merciful parent, seen in Athena, goddess of wisdom and justice. Moiseiwitsch's designs evoked this world through stylized masks and contrasting statures of human beings, heroes, and gods. Ordinary mortals—the Chorus, Watchman, Messenger, Nurse, and Servants—were of normal stature; the heroic figures—Clytemnestra, Agamemnon, Orestes, Electra, and Aegisthus—were larger than life, about six and a half feet tall (fig. no. 99). Finally, the gods Athena, Apollo, and Hermes, at nine feet, majestically towered over all. The Furies, though human in scale, did not look human; faceless, dangerous creatures, they suggested decay and filth (fig. no. 100).

Moiseiwitsch was astonished by the actors' ability to perform difficult movements while masked: "Given practice [and] masks of lighter weight and better visibility, somehow the actors did…fantastic feats of endurance and strength."[8] Len Cariou, who played Orestes, said it was simply a matter of having sufficient rehearsal time—120 hours—with the elevated boots. Rather than waiting until dress rehearsal, "Tanya was certain from virtually the *first* rehearsal we had these boots, so I could walk around 'en point' in my cothurni by the end."[9] The boots were fabricated by the wardrobe staff, who fitted each actor individually. The taller shoes, requiring support above the ankle, were made by adding six inches of hard rubber to the soles of sport boots. Strapping and stylized sculpted toes concealed the leather shoes, transforming them into Greek cothurni. For the gods, stilts of lightweight metal

97

98

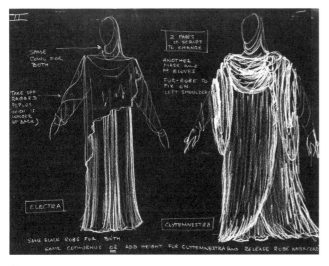

99

100

97. "Herakles," *Research Notebook* from *The House of Atreus*, 1967, cat. no. 93

98. "Greek Kouroi," *Research Notebook* from *The House of Atreus*, 1967, cat. no. 93

99. "Electra and Clytemnestra" *Costume Designs (Costume Room Copy)* from *The House of Atreus*, 1967, cat. no. 95 (photo: Guthrie Theater Archives, University of Minnesota Libraries, St. Paul)

100. "Leader of the Furies" *Costume Designs (Director's Copy)* from *The House of Atreus*, 1967, cat. no. 96 (photo: Guthrie Theater Archives, University of Minnesota Libraries, St. Paul)

tubing were attached to metal soles and strapped to the actors' feet. Balance was maintained with braces that strapped to the calves, and on the bottom of each stilt was a padded plywood base.

Moiseiwitsch created twenty-seven different designs which represented over eighty individual masks. All followed the form used earlier in *Oedipus Rex*, covering only the upper facial features, leaving the mouth and chin unobstructed. Carolyn Parker sculpted the lightweight masks with gauze and buckram layered over papier-mâché bits and sealed for painting. String, tow, and other materials were used as hair and beards. Stylized wigs, crowns, or helmets were incorporated into the masks of principal characters in much the same fashion as they had been for the masks of Jocasta, Oedipus, and Creon. Moiseiwitsch commented that "the masks made one realize that human personality is not exclusively expressed in the face." Their impassive quality, she explained, "emphasized all other means of expression," such as posture and rhythm, and the immobile masks lent a listening figure a powerful intensity.[10]

The great mask of Clytemnestra (fig. nos. 101–103, color plates 36, 38) allowed the actor Douglas Campbell to see through the cheek bones. The sculpted eyebrows were harrowed, the wide and noble brow was fringed with scarlet hair fashioned with two bands in a Greek-style coiffeur, and a smooth texture created an enameled look. The actor's mouth and chin were made up according to the designer's specifications: lips were burnt sienna, outlined with black. The mask for Aegisthus (fig. nos. 105, 106), played by Robert Pastene, was stony gray and the expression was to appear crafty, with angled brows and cheeks, and eyes that were slits, like Agamemnon's (fig. nos. 104, 107, color plates 31, 32). Moiseiwitsch wanted the texture to be "scrumbed and scritchy," as she noted in plans. To avoid too great a uniformity in the chorus (for the first play), three different types of masks were created for its fifteen members (fig. no. 108). Clytemnestra's four handmaidens were to be alike, with masks that echoed their mistress's features.

101

102

101. *Mask Design for Clytemnestra* from *The House of Atreus*, 1967, cat. 102

102. *Clytemnestra* from *The House of Atreus*, 1967, cat. no. 103

103. *Corpse's Head (Clytemnestra)* from *The House of Atreus*, 1967, cat. no. 113

104. *Agamemnon* from *The House of Atreus*, 1967, cat. no. 100

105. *Mask Design for Aegisthus* from *The House of Atreus*, 1967, cat. no. 99

106. *Mask of Aegisthus I* from *The House of Atreus*, 1967, cat. 107

107. *Mask of Agamemnon* from *The House of Atreus*, 1967, cat. no. 108

103

104

105

106

107

107

108. *Chorus Mask II* from *The House of Atreus*, 1967, cat. nos. 111, 112

109. *Mask* from *The House of Atreus*, 1967, cat. no. 115

Moiseiwitsch and costumier Annette Garceau further disguised the individuality of the actors with long-sleeved robes and carefully painted gloves to match the dresses. Sleeves were cut with loops that slid over the palm of the glove so that extending an arm would not accidently expose the skin. Similarly, hoods were attached to the chorus masks as they were in *Oedipus*, and some masks were equipped with a draped scarf or bib to hide the neck of the performer. The greater personages required enlarged hands created by adding long fingernails to the bigger gloves. Chest and shoulder pads, not unlike those worn in football, built up the actor's bodies to correspond with the increased proportions. Garments were fabricated from many bolts of very wide cloth of a type normally used by scenic technicians for cycloramas or scenic backdrops, and fabric strips were woven into webbed netting for dresses and cloaks. Clytemnestra's garment, for example, was built from hundreds of gray, lavender, and dark brown strips individually attached to netting so they could respond to motion independently. Because ease in movement was a primary consideration, Moiseiwitsch had to allow for sufficient leg room and pay special attention to long garments that might easily trip an "elevated" actor.

The designs for *The House of Atreus* have a primitive, painfully earthbound quality. Like titanic animated sculptures, the massive weathered figures looked as if they had survived the elements. Their pock-marked surfaces, meant to recall the ancient Greek ruins pictured in photographs Moiseiwitsch presented to her staff, were achieved by building up layers of spattered paint and dyes. Tiny dots of color created the effect of corrosion—quite different from the *Oedipus* costumes, which had been dyed or painted along folds to emphasize highlights and shadows or to accent specific decorative details. Moiseiwitsch's color scheme grew in part from research into archaic and classical Greek art. The flat orange and blue on the soldiers' helmets (fig. no. 110, color plate 34) was derived from pottery painting. The sun god, Apollo, was gold gilt, and had Mycenaean resonances, his face

110. *Helmet* from *The House of Atreus*, 1967, cat. no. 114

111. *Armor* from *The House of Atreus*, 1967, cat. no. 109

like a disc, sneering and blistered, with oxlike eyes. Hermes was pewter with silver highlights, and Pallas Athena, inspired by a pink Parian marble, was matte and semi-smooth with a stern stare which was also wise (fig. nos. 112–114, color plates 33, 35). The Furies were grotesque, faceless masks and shapeless bodies in black. But the predominant colors were "browns like dried clay, and reds like caked blood."[11]

Moiseiwitsch simplified the setting for all three plays in this condensed *Oresteia*. Two eighteen-foot doors with massive rings for handles represented the tomb, palace, and shrines. At one point, the door swung open to reveal Pallas Athena on her throne. The seated statue appeared to be living marble; from inside this huge figure of justice, Campbell actually stood and could turn and tilt the head, and by manipulating rods inside, he could also dramatically gesture with the long arm in the closing scene when Orestes pleads for his life. The grand scale of the production suited the space and the asymmetrical thrust stage in Minneapolis extraordinarily well, according to an eye witness who paid tribute to Moiseiwitsch's talent for coordinating the proportions of the playing space with the design.[12]

Her design for *The House of Atreus* was honored by the Los Angeles Drama Circle and the New York Drama Critics in 1968. Following this success, Moiseiwitsch would design other masked Greek dramas, building on the conventions furthered in this production. For the Crucible Theatre in Sheffield, Moiseiwitsch designed Aeschylus's *The Persians* in 1972, directed by Colin George, and for the South Australia Theatre Company in Adelaide she would realize Sophocles' *Oedipus Rex* and *Oedipus at Colonus* with the same director in 1978. The adaptor of the Greek drama in each case was John Lewin, who had also transformed the Oresteian trilogy into *The House of Atreus*. In the ensuing years, *The House of Atreus* has remained Moiseiwitsch's most spectacular, legendary, and powerful masked production, "a rite, an evocation of something high and formidable, an image of magnificence."[13]

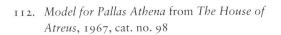

112

113

114

115

116

112. *Model for Pallas Athena* from *The House of Atreus*, 1967, cat. no. 98

113. *Athena* from *The House of Atreus*, 1967, cat. no. 101

114. *Head of Pallas Athena* from *The House of Atreus*, 1967, cat. no. 110

115. *Mask Design for the Eumenides* from *The House of Atreus*, 1967, cat. no. 104

116. *Three of the Eumenides* from *The House of Atreus*, 1967, cat. no. 105

NOTES

1. James Forsyth, *Tyrone Guthrie, A Biography* (London: Hamish Hamilton, 1976), 294; Mel Gussow, "Minneapolis on Broadway," *Newsweek*, 6 January 1969, 57; Henry Popkin, "Aeschylus Draws Packed Houses in Minneapolis," *New York Times*, 18 October 1967.

2. Tyrone Guthrie eloquently describes this theory in *A Life in the Theatre* (New York: McGraw-Hill, 1959), 349–50, and expands upon it in chapter two of *In Various Directions* (New York: Macmillan, 1965).

3. Robertson Davies, Tanya Moiseiwitsch, Tyrone Guthrie, et al., *Thrice the Brinded Cat Hath Mew'd* (Toronto: Clarke, Irvin, and Co., 1955), 123, 124–25. Moiseiwitsch and Guthrie offer a highly informative explanation and description of this production as a chapter in this unique volume; see esp. 111–78.

4. Tanya Moiseiwitsch, interviewed by Alfred Rossi, *Astonish Us in the Morning* (Detroit: Wayne State University Press, 1980), 54. Hereafter cited as "Rossi interview."

5. Tyrone Guthrie, preface, *Aeschylus, The House of Atreus: A Version for the Stage* (Minneapolis: Guthrie Theater, 1967), 10.

6. Julius Novick, "Theater," *The Nation*, 18 September 1967, 252.

7. Tyrone Guthrie, "The Director Comments," *Setting the Stage*, Fifth Season. A play guide prepared by Minnesota Theater Company, 1967, Guthrie Theater Archives, University of Minnesota.

8. Rossi interview, 54.

9. Len Cariou, interviewed by the author, New York, November 1979.

10. Moiseiwitsch in Davies et al., *Thrice the Brinded Cat*, 133.

11. Daniel Sullivan, "Guthrie Theater Opens Adaptation of Trilogy," *New York Times*, 23 July 1967.

12. When the production traveled, however, some felt the theaters' architecture detracted from its success. Cariou, in the interview cited above, told me that the smaller auditorium of the Mark Taper Forum in Los Angeles brought the audience too close to the thrust stage and the production style tended to overwhelm: "It simply needed more space aesthetically." The proscenium stage of the Broadway Billy Rose Theatre cramped the production even more, confining movement to a flat plane. The dynamic sweep of massive figures in space and the sculptural effect of the costumes were greatly reduced on the proscenium stage, with its picture frame.

13. Novick, "Theater," 254.

Guthrie Theater
Minneapolis, 1967
Directed by Tyrone Guthrie

93
Research Notebook
Pencil, watercolor on paper, 14 x 11 3/4 x 1/2
(35.6 x 29.8 x 1), closed
On loan to the Stratford Festival, Canada, from
the Guthrie Theater Archives, University of
Minnesota Libraries, St. Paul

94*
Costume Designs (Design Room Copy)
Duplicate drawings, fabric swatches,
18 x 24 1/2 (45.7 x 62.2), sheet
Guthrie Theater Archives, University of
Minnesota Libraries, St. Paul
Chicago and Minneapolis venues only

95
Costume Designs (Costume Room Copy)
Duplicate drawings,
18 x 24 1/2 (45.7 x 62.2), sheet
Guthrie Theater Archives, University of
Minnesota Libraries, St. Paul
Chicago and Minneapolis venues only

96
Costume Designs (Director's Copy)
Duplicate drawings,
18 x 24 1/2 (45.7 x 62.2), sheet
Guthrie Theater Archives, University of
Minnesota Libraries, St. Paul
Chicago and Minneapolis venues only

97*
Scrapbook
Black-and-white photographs, newspaper
clippings, 12 7/16 x 10 3/8 x 3/8
(31.6 x 26.3 x 1), closed
On loan to the Stratford Festival, Canada, from
the Guthrie Theater Archives, University of
Minnesota Libraries, St. Paul

98
Model for Pallas Athena (Douglas Campbell)
Wood, wire, cheesecloth, string, papier mâché,
cardboard, paint, 11 x 3 3/4 (27.9 x 9.5)
Courtesy of Annette Garceau

99
Mask Design for Aegisthus (Robert Pastene)
Pencil, brush and ink, red felt marker on paper,
7 3/4 x 11 3/4 (19.7 x 29.8), image
Private collection, James and Gail Bakkom,
Minneapolis

100
Agamemnon (Lee Richardson)
Pencil, watercolor, gouache on paper,
16 1/4 x 22 3/8 (41.3 x 56.8), image
Courtesy of Moira Wylie

101
Athena
Pen and ink, acrylic on paper,
16 7/8 x 11 3/4 (42.9 x 29.8)
Courtesy of Annette Garceau

102
Mask Design for Clytemnestra
(Douglas Campbell)
Pencil, brush and ink, red felt marker on paper,
17 5/8 x 11 3/4 (44.8 x 29.8), image
Private collection, James and Gail Bakkom,
Minneapolis

103
Clytemnestra
Watercolor, gouache, metallic paint on paper,
16 x 10 1/2 (40.7 x 26.7), image
Courtesy of Moira Wylie

104
Mask Design for the Eumenides
Acrylic, brush and ink, pencil on paper,
16 1/4 x 12 1/16 (41.3 x 30.6)
Tanya Moiseiwitsch Collection

105
Three of the Eumenides
Acrylic, white pencil, brush and ink on paper,
12 3/8 x 9 13/16 (31.4 x 24.9)
Tanya Moiseiwitsch Collection

106*
Libation Kylix
Pencil, ballpoint pen, watercolor, felt marker
on paper, 8 7/8 x 17 3/16 (22.6 x 43.7)
Private collection, James and Gail Bakkom,
Minneapolis

107
Mask of Aegisthus I
Papier mâché, gauze, string, tobacco cloth,
paint, 22 1/2 x 14 3/8 (57.2 x 36.5)
Guthrie Theater Costume Collection,
Minneapolis

108
Mask of Agamemnon
Papier mâché, construction paper, glue, paint,
polymer medium, bronzing powders, felt, wire,
22 x 12 (55.9 x 30.5)
Private collection, James and Gail Bakkom,
Minneapolis

109
Armor
Fiberglass, paint, 22 1/2 x 14 (57.2 x 35.6)
Private collection, James and Gail Bakkom,
Minneapolis

110
Head of Pallas Athena
Celastic, cheesecloth, acrylic paint, satin fabric,
38 x 14 x 27 (96.5 x 35.5 x 68.6)
Guthrie Theater Costume Collection,
Minneapolis

111
Chorus Mask II (Mr. Swartz)
Papier mâché, wire, tobacco cloth, polymer,
glue, latex paint, 9 1/4 x 7 3/4 x 5
(23.5 x 19.7 x 12.7)
Private collection

112
Chorus Mask II (Miss Harrelson)
Papier mâché, wire, tobacco cloth, polymer,
glue, latex paint, 9 1/4 x 7 7/8 (23.5 x 20)
Private collection, James and Gail Bakkom,
Minneapolis

113
Corpse's Head (Clytemnestra)
Cellular foam, cheesecloth, glue, latex, jute
netting, shellac, 48 x 24 (121.9 x 60.9)
Guthrie Theater Costume Collection,
Minneapolis

114
Helmet
fiberglass, flexible glue, paint, 26 x 10
(66 x 25.5)
Private collection, James and Gail Bakkom,
Minneapolis

115
Mask
Papier mâché, construction paper, glue, paint,
polymer medium, bronzing powders, felt, wire,
15 3/4 x 10 7/16 (40 x 26.4)
Private collection, James and Gail Bakkom,
Minneapolis

Douglas Campbell as Pallas Athena, Lee Richardson as Apollo, and Len Cariou as Orestes in *The House of Atreus*, Guthrie Theater, Minneapolis, 1967 (photo: Don Getsug Studios)

Lee Richardson as Agamemnon and Len Cariou as
Orestes in *The House of Atreus*, Guthrie Theater,
Minneapolis, 1967 (photo: Don Getsug Studios)

Guthrie said, "Well, now, Apollo, you know, ought to be about nine foot tall." Well, looking at him, I could see that nine feet just meant a few inches above his head. "All very well for you. But think of the actor going up that high. Is he going to have to walk about?" "Oh, yes, yes." Mostly they were built cothurni, which were based on what we did at Stratford for Oedipus. They worked at Stratford—Douglas Campbell, who was in both productions, knew they'd work. But when we were asked to go up to a certain height beyond that, Gordon Smith, the production manager, one day came into the wardrobe, where everyone was busy sewing, with their heads down, busy, and they looked up and they saw him walking about, and thought, he's just checking, and then someone said, "Oh, he's very tall." He was walking on one-foot-six extensions under his shoes, which were called plasterer's stilts. They're commercial, you buy them in the shops. He was lent a pair, he went scouting around for ideas, and no obligation to purchase if it didn't work. He walked around with people not noticing he was walking in any other way except he was very tall. Of course one actor, the man who played Apollo, Lee Richardson, had to be coerced into trying them on. The first few steps were very tentative. He was holding on to two people, he let go, and he started to walk. They had kind of flexible feet at the very bottom, so you didn't have to stomp as on real stilts. Then everyone wanted to have a go. They were all putting them on. So one pair was bought and heavily decorated with gold paint and fattened up to look like a boot.

Also adapted from an interview by Arnold Wengrow, *The Journal for Design and Production Professionals in the Performing Arts* 28 (Fall 1992).

Lee Richardson as Agamemnon and Robin Gammell as Cassandra in *The House of Atreus*, Guthrie Theater, Minneapolis, 1967 (photo: Don Getsug Studios)

Phaedra Britannica

National Theatre at the Old Vic
London, 1975

THE BRITISH PRESS STORMED when the National Theatre of Great Britain's *Phaedra Britannica* opened at the Old Vic in September 1975. Some hailed Tony Harrison's updated version of the Phaedra story as a bolt of genius, while others condemned him for having taken a crowbar to Jean Racine's classic. The controversy made *Phaedra* the talk of London, and eventually of New York, where the production was transferred for a limited engagement the following year. Bringing together Harrison, director John Dexter, actress Diana Rigg, and designer Tanya Moiseiwitsch, all of whom had collaborated on *The Misanthrope*, the National's most conspicuous success in two seasons, *Phaedra Britannica* raised a lot of issues, not to mention eyebrows.

The idea of placing the action in British colonial India just prior to the Indian Mutiny in the 1840s was established before Moiseiwitsch was brought onto the project. Over her four decades as a theatrical designer, however, she had transposed many classical texts into different epochs, whether to present a specific point of view, create a desired illusion, or elucidate difficult plot points. She had devised a romantic Byronic world for *Twelfth Night*, placed *As You Like It* among the plantations of the antebellum South, and updated plays by Molière and Ben Jonson to the 1960s. "Every decade has a different way," said Moiseiwitsch, "and there's no turning back the pages and saying this is *the* way it was done in 1602—plays are not museum replicas."[1] She understood that the selection of period ultimately depends on the director and his or her interpretation. Is it to be pictorial, experimental, playful, or dark?

A prevailing consideration, according to Moiseiwitsch, is always to make the cast look appealing and convincing in their roles, so that the choice between short skirts and long dresses, for example, may be tempered by the shape of the leading lady. Obviously there are other grounds for such decisions. Moiseiwitsch

recalled that director Tyrone Guthrie once intended to send up the army in *All's Well That Ends Well*; dressing the soldiers in Edwardian puttees brightened the humor of the play. The *Hamlet* performed at the Guthrie Theater in Minneapolis in 1963 had the look of a European court before World War I for an entirely different reason. Royal occasions with men in ceremonial uniform and women in long skirts and gloves "even now do not suggest any specific date," wrote Guthrie, who noted advantages of costuming the play in modern attire.[2] Characters looked more real, he argued, more picturesque than in period dress; economic and social rank were more easily conveyed.

Moiseiwitsch's contemporary design for the National Theatre's *Misanthrope*, which won her a Tony award nomination when it was produced in New York in 1975, was described by the *Times of London* as elegant, chic, and glossy.[3] Her striking contrast between setting and costumes inaugurated the production with an irresistible *coup de théâtre*, according to *Punch* magazine, whose reviewer described the opening scene:

> The curtain rises upon a faintly lit stage; stiffly voluminous silvery drapes hang above an unlit chandelier suggestive of baroque swathes that frame portraits of Louis XIV. A figure sits with his back to a classical facade, listening to some twiddly string music. One prepares oneself for an evening of seventeenth-century brocade. Enter the first character who switches on the chandelier, switches off the record player, and we are in a smartly furnished *beau monde* of 1966.[4]

For *Phaedra*, Harrison rejected both the traditional settings of Racine's seventeenth-century France and of Euripides' classical Greece, "since both locations," he believed, "have too many distorting mirrors." In his search for a level of language and an appropriate milieu in which to place his play, he was struck by an image of Phaedra stretched out in a closed room in a country where the sun was exploding. Harrison "began to think about

India . . . [and] gradually it became clear that Phaedra's confidante could be her Ayah, and slowly it all began to fit."[5] Theseus became the governor, played by Michael Gough, and Phaedra the governor's wife, Memsahib, performed by Diana Rigg. Hippolytus, renamed Thomas Theophilus, played by David Yelland, was the governor's son by his first wife, a Rajput princess. To unify time and action, Harrison placed the entourage within the official governor's residence, protected from the hostile jungle and a rebellious people influenced by foreign gods.

When researching historical fashion, Moiseiwitsch relied on art museums and their libraries for paintings and for books of fashion plates of the era. Steeping herself in visual material contemporary to the play's period, Moiseiwitsch found creative stimulation. Sometimes her research focused on a particular character in the play, or "the way soldiers wore their swords, or the colors that were really used" at the time. The application of this research to the final design did not occur in any specific order. "It's rather like stirring up ingredients for a pudding and you have to refer to the recipe several times," quipped Moiseiwitsch. The research served as an inspiration for the design, "but it's only part of the job," she continued. "Next is to get the characters of the play onto paper. I don't mean you just trace a print that you've seen and put a character's name on it. They have to be reinterpreted—translated to the stage—and of course the director has a big say in that."[6]

Dexter was guided by his view that the Phaedra myth is about sexual denial. "The wife who says 'I love you' to her stepson . . . has the feeling of saying something forbidden and [is] feeling guilty every moment. . . . It is a basic human situation about people who resist their sexuality." In India, the colonial rulers emphasized law, order, and reason. Just beyond the walls of the governor's residence, however, was the jungle and "the enormous sensuality of India expressed in erotic paintings, the attitude to sex was freer and more embracing. The English felt it had to be kept out."[7] Moiseiwitsch communicated this restrictive attitude in her designs. Rigg's tightly corseted profile as the Memsahib, with her

117. "Amah," *Research Notebook* from *Phaedra Britannica*, 1975, cat. no. 116

118. *The Governor in Disguise* from *Phaedra Britannica*, 1975, cat. no. 122

119. *Thomas Theophilus* from *Phaedra Britannica*, 1975, cat. no. 127

120. *The Memsahib* from *Phaedra Britannica*, 1975, cat. no. 124

121. *The Memsahib, Act 2, scenes 6 and 8* from *Phaedra Britannica*, 1975, cat. no. 126

high-buttoned collar and voluminous skirt and shawl (fig. nos. 120, 121, color plate 44), bespoke English Victorian propriety and denied the steaming tropical sexual atmosphere. The neatly tailored military uniforms (fig. no. 122) underscored the British imperial presence, about to ignite with the civil unrest hanging in the air. Tara's and Ayah's loose flowing native saris (fig. no. 123) heighten this cultural and societal contrast.

The stage set, with its sweeping colonnade representing the portico of the governor's residence, echoed the classical Greek origins of the Phaedra legend. Brown and beige were the dominating colors of the stage picture, creating a mood that was both austere and stifling. Counterpoised on either side of the stage were His Excellency's ornate audience room with its throne of power, and opposite, mounted over the arched entry, the bronze image of the Hindu deity Shiva, destroyer and creator. Moiseiwitsch's sketch (fig. no. 126, color plate 40) is actually an early version of the design, and omits the slatted blinds, which prevented the outside world from intruding into the governor's halls (fig. no. 127, color plate 41). In the final climactic moments of the play, when Memsahib crumbles into a heap and expires, the threatening monsoons hit, rattling these slats with howling wind and torrential rains. Distilling scenic art to its dramatic essence, Moiseiwitsch's designs for *Phaedra Britannica* won praise from all quarters; one drama critic who reviewed the production referred to her as "the doyenne, and quite possibly the best of British stage designers."[8]

This production raises the provocative and not easily answered question of how the classics of literature should be presented on contemporary stages. As historically accurate replicas of

120

122. *A.D.C. to the Governor* from *Phaedra Britannica,*
1975, cat. no. 119

123. *Ayah* from *Phaedra Britannica,* 1975, cat. no. 120

124. *Burleigh* from *Phaedra Britannica,* 1975, cat.
no. 121

125. *Lilamani* from *Phaedra Britannica,* 1975,
cat. no. 123

122

123

124

125

126. *Set Design* from *Phaedra Britannica*, 1975, cat. no. 117

127. *Set Model* from *Phaedra Britannica*, 1975, cat. no. 118

the period in which they were written? Or as stories that, having stood the test of time, throb with contemporary meaning, probing our human condition? "Modern dress," wrote Alec Guinness, "will often breathe fresh air on an old play and give it a fair chance of revaluation, firmly pointing out how little the human heart changes through the centuries, and how remarkably alike we are to our forebears."[9] Moreover, those who demand their Shakespeare in Elizabethan pumpkin pants, or their Racine in togas, should be reminded that until the nineteenth century, most Shakespeare was performed in contemporary dress. Charles Kemble's *King John* (1823), William Charles McCready's *Coriolanus* (1838), and Charles Kean's *King John* (1852) startled London theater-goers with painstakingly historical reproduction, linking the past, through scholarly research, with theatrical presentation. Shakespeare himself, however, seemed notoriously indifferent to historical accuracy. His Romans, for instance, refer to clocks, buttons on their togas, and Elizabethan rapiers. Anachronisms abound.

Well into the last quarter of the nineteenth century, actors were commonly required to provide their own costumes. The

touring star or actor/manager could be recognized by his elaborate attention-drawing accoutrements. In resident stock companies until that time, actors and theatrical costumers generally recognized three periods—Roman, Shakespearean, and Old Comedy, with white wigs and knee breeches characterizing the last. Little historical or artistic congruity in costuming was practiced; and the theater scene designer was either an architect or a painter—scene design was only a sideline. According to noted theatrical historian and scholar Orville Larson, it was "not until the organic theory of production [that] the scenic artist became an artist in his own right, devoting himself exclusively to the theater."[10]

The organic theory, developed prior to World War I, fused all the elements of a theatrical production into a unified artistic whole in accordance with the demands of the script. The influential writings of Edward Gordon Craig, Adolphe Appia, and Granville-Barker's productions of Shakespeare and George Bernard Shaw were instrumental in this evolution. Moiseiwitsch was one of the first artists in Britain to be a purveyor of the theory as well as an avid and prodigious practitioner. In *Phaedra Britannica*, in which the "Euripidean sense of tragic devastation found a new home in the hot, torn beauty of India's landscape,"[11] Moiseiwitsch demonstrated once again her willingness to transfer a dramatic masterpiece to another time and locale, exploring resonance of meaning in a seamless collaboration that was true to the spirit of the classical text.

NOTES

1. Tanya Moiseiwitsch, "The Director and the Designer," International Lecture Series panel discussion with Herbert Whittaker and Murry Lauffer, Ontario College of Art, 24 May 1979. Stratford Festival Archives, Ontario.

2. Tyrone Guthrie, "Hamlet in Modern Dress," *Drama Survey*, 3 (Spring-Summer 1963): 73.

3. Irving Wardle, "Satisfying Molière in New Translation: *Misanthrope* National," *Times of London*, 23 February 1973.

4. Jeremy Kingston, "Theater," *Punch*, 7 March 1973.

5. Tony Harrison, interviewed by Sheridan Morely, "Tony Harrison Turns Phaedre into Memsahib," *The Times Saturday Review*, 6 September 1975.

6. Tanya Moiseiwitsch, interviewed by Sheldon Goldstein, "Backstage at the Guthrie," Radio WLOL-FM, Tape 27, broadcast 14 June 1965. Guthrie Theater Archives, University of Minnesota.

7. John Dexter and Diana Rigg, interviewed in "The Exorcism of Miss Rigg," *The Evening Standard*, 5 September 1975.

8. Robert Cushman, "Hail Britannica," *Observer*, 14 September 1975.

9. Alec Guinness, "Shakespeare in Modern Dress," Stratford Festival Program, 1953, n.p. Stratford Festival Archives, Ontario.

10. Orville K. Larson, *Scene Design for Stage and Screen, Readings on the Aesthetics and Methodology of Scene Design for Drama, Opera, Musical Comedy, Ballet, Motion Pictures, Television and Area Theater*, (Westport, Conn.: Greenwood Press, 1961), ix.

11. Clive Barnes, "Stage: Old Vic's 'Phèdre,'" *New York Times*, 10 September 1975.

PHAEDRA BRITANNICA

National Theatre at the Old Vic
London, 1975
Directed by John Dexter

116
Research Notebook, 1974-75
Pencil on paper, 13 5/8 x 10 x 1
(34.6 x 25.5 x 2.5), closed
Tanya Moiseiwitsch Collection

117
Set Design
Pen and ink, wash on paper,
15 9/16 x 22 5/8 (39.5 x 57.4)
Tanya Moiseiwitsch Collection

118
Set Model
Mat board, balsa wood, gouache, wire, papier
mâché, contact paper, metallic paint, fabric,
15 1/2 x 22 1/2 (39.4 x 57.2)
Tanya Moiseiwitsch Collection

119
A.D.C. to the Governor (Daniel Thorndike)
Acrylic, white pencil, glitter on paper,
18 x 11 7/8 (45.7 x 30.2)
Tanya Moiseiwitsch Collection

120
Ayah (Alaknanda Samarth)
Acrylic, white pencil on paper,
17 7/8 x 11 7/8 (45.4 x 30.2)
The Stratford Festival, Canada

121
Burleigh (Robert Eddison)
Acrylic, watercolor, brush and ink, white pencil
on paper, 17 15/16 x 12 (45.5 x 30.4)
Tanya Moiseiwitsch Collection

122
The Governor in Disguise (Michael Gough)
Acrylic, white pencil on paper,
17 7/8 x 11 7/8 (45.4 x 30.2)
The Stratford Festival, Canada

123
Lilamani (Diana Quick)
Acrylic, white pencil, glitter on paper,
18 x 11 15/16 (45.7 x 30.4)
Tanya Moiseiwitsch Collection

124
The Memsahib (Diana Rigg)
Acrylic, white pencil on paper,
17 15/16 x 11 7/8 (45.5 x 30.2)
Tanya Moiseiwitsch Collection

125*
The Memsahib, Act 1, Scene 2
Acrylic, white pencil on paper,
17 7/8 x 11 7/8 (45.4 x 30.2)
The Stratford Festival, Canada

126
The Memsahib, Act 2, Scenes 6 and 8
Acrylic, white pencil, glitter on paper,
17 15/16 x 11 15/16 (45.6 x 30.3)
Tanya Moiseiwitsch Collection

127
Thomas Theophilus (David Yelland)
Acrylic, white pencil on paper,
17 15/16 x 11 15/16 (45.5 x 30.3)
Tanya Moiseiwitsch Collection

Diana Rigg as the Memsahib, Alaknanda Samarth as Ayah, and Daniel Thorndike as Aide-de-Camp in *Phaedra Britannica*, National Theatre at the Old Vic, London, 1975 (photo: Anthony Crickmay. Collections of the Theatre Museum. By courtesy of the Board of Trustees of the Victoria and Albert Museum, London)

Alaknanda Samarth as Ayah and Diana Rigg as the Memsahib in *Phaedra Britannica*, National Theatre at the Old Vic, London, 1975 (photo: Anthony Crickmay. Collections of the Theatre Museum. By courtesy of the Board of Trustees of the Victoria and Albert Museum, London)

Chronology

Information for each production is listed as follows: opening date, title of play, author, director, and company/theater. A complete list of theaters and their shortened names used below follows the chronology.

1934

17 December, *The Faithful*, John Masefield, Norman Page, Royal Academy of Dramatic Arts (RADA)/Westminster

20 December, *Alien Corn*, Sidney Howard, Norman Page, RADA/Westminster

1935–38

Costumer and designer for various productions in weekly repertory at the Abbey Theatre, including:

Church Street, Lennox Robinson, Hugh Hunt, Abbey

Damer's Gold, Lady Augusta Gregory, Hugh Hunt

Dervorgilla, Lady Augusta Gregory, Hugh Hunt

The Plough and the Stars, Sean O'Casey, Hugh Hunt

The Shadowy Waters, W. B. Yeats, Hugh Hunt

Shewing up of Blanco Posnet, G. B. Shaw, Hugh Hunt

Thomas Muskerry, Padraic Colum, Hugh Hunt

The Well of the Saints, J. M. Synge, Hugh Hunt

The Words upon the Window Pane, W. B. Yeats, (?)

1935

16 September, *A Deuce o' Jacks*, F. R. Higgins, Michael J. Dolan, Abbey

14 October, *Parnell of Avondale*, W. R. Fearon, Lennox Robinson, Abbey

30 October, *Candida*, G. B. Shaw, Hugh Hunt, Abbey

30 October, *Village Wooing*, G. B. Shaw, Hugh Hunt, Abbey

4 November, *Noah*, André Obey, Hugh Hunt, Abbey

2 December, *A Saint in a Hurry*, José María Pemán, Lennox Robinson, Abbey

9 December, *Summer's Day*, Maura Molloy, Hugh Hunt, Abbey

1936

13 January, *Coriolanus*, William Shakespeare, Hugh Hunt, Abbey

2 February, *The Grand House in the City*, Brinsley McNamara, Hugh Hunt, Abbey

24 February, *Boyd's Shop*, St. John Ervine, Hugh Hunt, Abbey

16 March, *Katie Roche*, Teresa Deevy, Hugh Hunt, Abbey

13 April, *The Passing Day*, George Shiels, Hugh Hunt, Abbey

1 June, *Hassan*, James Elroy Flecker, Hugh Hunt, Abbey

27 July, *The Playboy of the Western World*, J. M. Synge, Hugh Hunt, Abbey

10 August, *Deirdre*, W. B. Yeats, Hugh Hunt, Abbey

14 September, *The Silver Jubilee*, Cormac O'Daly, Hugh Hunt, Abbey

12 October, *The Jailbird*, George Shiels, Hugh Hunt, Abbey

2 November, *Fanny's First Play*, G. B. Shaw, Lennox Robinson (?), Abbey

9 November, *The Wild Goose*, Teresa Deevy, Hugh Hunt, Abbey

30 November, *Wind from the West*, Maeve O'Callaghan, Hugh Hunt, Abbey

26 December, *Blind Man's Buff*, Ernst Toller and Denis Johnston, Hugh Hunt, Abbey

1937

25 January, *Shadow and Substance*, Paul Vincent Carroll, Hugh Hunt, Abbey. Revived 1 August 1938.

8 February, *The End of the Beginning*, Sean O'Casey, Arthur Shields, Abbey

29 March, *Quin's Secret*, George Shiels, Hugh Hunt, Abbey. Revived 24 October 1938.

19 April, *Killycreggs in Twilight*, Lennox Robinson, Hugh Hunt, Abbey

17 May, *Who Will Remember…?*, Maura Molloy, Hugh Hunt, Abbey

31 May, *In the Train*, Frank O'Connor and Hugh Hunt, Hugh Hunt, Abbey

5 August, *The Patriot*, Maeve O'Callaghan, Hugh Hunt, Abbey

31 August, *The Lost Leader*, Lennox Robinson, Hugh Hunt, Abbey

27 September, *The Man in the Cloak*, Louis D'Alton, Hugh Hunt, Abbey

18 October, *The Invincibles*, Hugh Hunt and Frank O'Connor, Hugh Hunt, Abbey. Revived 4 August 1938.

8 November, *Cartney and Kevney*, George Shiels, Hugh Hunt (?), Abbey

22 November, *Coggerers*, Paul Vincent Carroll, Hugh Hunt, Abbey

1938

17 January, *Neal Maquade*, George Shiels, Hugh Hunt, Abbey

14 February, *A Spot in the Sun*, T. C. Murray, Hugh Hunt, Abbey

24 February, *Moses' Rock*, Hugh Hunt and Frank O'Connor, Abbey

4 April, *The Dear Queen*, Andrew Ganly, Hugh Hunt, Abbey

9 May, *Casadh an t'Súgáin*, Douglas Hyde, Hugh Hunt, Abbey

(?) May, *The Well of the Saints*, J. M. Synge, Hugh Hunt, Abbey

25 July, *The Moon in the Yellow River*, Denis Johnston, Hugh Hunt, Abbey

12 September, *Bird's Nest*, Lennox Robinson, Hugh Hunt, Abbey

19 September, *The Great Adventure*, Charles I. Foley, Hugh Hunt, Abbey

10 October, *Pilgrims*, Mary Rynne, Hugh Hunt, Abbey

12 December, *Baintighearna an Ghorta*, Seamus Wilmot, Prionnsias MacDiarmada, Abbey

26 December, *Time's Pocket*, Frank O'Connor, Prionnsias MacDiarmada, Abbey

1939

12 June, *The Plough and the Stars*, Sean O'Casey, Hugh Hunt, Q

3 July, *The Plough and the Stars*, Sean O'Casey, Hugh Hunt, Embassy

1940

2 January, *The Golden Cuckoo*, Denis Johnston, Hugh Hunt, Duchess

11 March, *They Knew What They Wanted*, Sidney Howard, Henry Cass, Q

1 April, *Temporary Residence*, Cyril Campion, Anthony Hawtrey, Q

8 April, *Cash and Carry*, Robert Brenon and Ray McLoughlin, Peter Dearing, Q

15 April, *Apple Sauce*, Richard Mainwaring and Stratton Taylor, Frank Gregory, Q

22 April, *A Lady Reflects*, Louis Verneuil and Georges Barr, Gwen Farrar, Q

29 April, *Passing By*, William Douglas Home, Noël Howlett, Q

6 May, *Quiet Wedding*, Esther McCracken, Peggie Dear, Q

13 May, *Saloon Bar*, Frank Harvey, Jr., Peter Dearing, Q

3 June, *House Party*, Anthony Booth, Jevan Brandon-Thomas, Q

10 June, *The Comic Artist*, Susan Glaspell and Norman Matson, Henry Cass, Q

24 June, *The School for Husbands*, F. Jackson, Jevan Brandon-Thomas, Q

8 July, *High Temperature*, Avery Hopwood and Wilson Collison, Jack Livsey, Q

25 July, *High Temperature*, Avery Hopwood and Wilson Collison, Henry Kendall, Duke of York/Comedy

5 August, *Outward Bound*, Sutton Vane, Irene Hentschell, Q

12 August, *Clive of India*, W. P. Lipscomb and R. J. Minney, Peter Dearing, Q

30 August, *Outward Bound*, Sutton Vane, Irene Hentschell, New

1941–44

Costumer and designer for various productions in weekly repertory at Oxford Playhouse, including:

Androcles and the Lion, G. B. Shaw, Peter Ashmore

Charley's Aunt, B. Thomas

Desire under the Elms, Eugene O'Neill

The Doctor's Dilemma, G. B. Shaw, Peter Ashmore

Fresh Fields, Ivor Novello

The Gentle People, Irwin Shaw, Peter Ashmore

George and Margaret, Gerald Savory, Peter Ashmore

Goodness, How Sad!, Robert Morley, Peter Ashmore

Guilty, Emile Zola

Is Life Worth Living?, Lennox Robinson

Jane Eyre; Charlotte Brontë, adapted by Helen Jerome

Jupiter Laughs, A. J. Cronin

The Little Foxes, Lillian Hellman

Lot's Wife, P. Blackmore

Love on the Dole, R. Gow and W. Greenwood

The Master Builder, Henrik Ibsen

The Merchant of Venice, William Shakespeare, Peter Ashmore

Misalliance, G. B. Shaw

Parnell, E. T. Schauffler

Quiet Wedding, Esther McCracken

Rain, Somerset W. Maugham

Rebecca, Daphne Du Maurier

Romeo and Juliet, William Shakespeare, Peter Ashmore

Rope, Patrick Hamilton, Peter Ashmore

The Seagull, Anton Chekhov

Sweeney Todd, the Barber of Fleet Street, Frederick Hazleton, Peter Ashmore

When We Are Married, J. B. Priestly

Wuthering Heights; Emily Brontë, adapted by R. Carter

1944

(?), *The Alchemist*, Ben Jonson, Tyrone Guthrie, Old Vic/Liverpool

(?), *Doctor Faustus*, Christopher Marlowe, John Moody, Old Vic/Liverpool

(?), *John Gabriel Borkman*, Henrik Ibsen, Peter Glenville, Old Vic/Liverpool

1945

(?), *The School for Scandal*, Richard Brinsley Sheridan, Peter Glenville, Old Vic/Liverpool

(?), *Point Valaine*, Noel Coward, Peter Glenville, Old Vic/Liverpool

16 January, *Uncle Vanya*, Anton Chekov, John Burrell, Old Vic/New

(?) February, *Hamlet*, William Shakespeare, Peter Ashmore, Old Vic/Liverpool

18 October, *The Critic or a Tragedy Rehearsed*, Richard Brinsley Sheridan, Miles Malleson, Old Vic/New

1946

14 February, *The Time of Your Life*, William Saroyan, Peter Glenville, Company of Four/Lyric

19 February, *The Beaux' Stratagem*, George Farquhar, Hugh Hunt, Old Vic/Bristol

5 June, *Twelfth Night*, William Shakespeare, Hugh Hunt, Old Vic/Bristol

26 June, *Weep for the Cyclops*, Denis Johnston, Hugh Hunt, Old Vic/Bristol (designed with Guy Sheppard)

24 October, *Cyrano de Bergerac*, Edmond Rostand, Tyrone Guthrie, Old Vic/New

1947

26 April; *Bless the Bride*; A. P. Herbert, music by Vivien Ellis; Wendy Toye; Adelphi

1 September, *Point Valaine*, Noel Coward, Peter Glenville, Embassy

6 November; *Peter Grimes*; Benjamin Britten, text by Montagu Slater; Tyrone Guthrie; Royal Opera House

1948

1 March, *Frenzy*, Peter Ustinov, Murray MacDonald, Royal Newcastle

17 March, *Lady Rohesia*, Antony Hopkins, Geoffrey Dunn, Sadler's Wells

21 April, *Frenzy*, Peter Ustinov, Murray MacDonald, St. Martin's

24 May; *The Beggar's Opera*; John Gay, realized by Benjamin Britten; Tyrone Guthrie; English Opera Group/Arts in Cambridge, Aldeburgh, Sadler's Wells, People's Palace

25 November, *The Cherry Orchard*, Anton Chekhov, Hugh Hunt, Old Vic/New

1949

11 July; *Bless the Bride*; A. P. Herbert, music by Vivien Ellis; Wendy Toye; tour beginning at Davis

15 July, *Henry VIII*, William Shakespeare, Tyrone Guthrie, Shakespeare

14 September, *Treasure Hunt*, M. J. Farrell and John Perry, John Gielgud, Apollo

25 October, *Don Giovanni*, W. A. Mozart, Geoffrey Dunn, Sadler's Wells

30 November, *A Month in the Country*, Ivan Turgenev, Michel Saint-Denis, Old Vic/New

1950

7 March, *Home at Seven*, R. C. Sherriff, Murray MacDonald, Wyndham's

28 March, *Henry VIII*, William Shakespeare, Tyrone Guthrie, Shakespeare (partly redesigned)

28 March, *The Holly and the Ivy*, Wynyard Brown, Frith Banbury, Lyric

10 May, *The Holly and the Ivy*, Wynyard Brown, Frith Banbury, Duchess

12 June, *Treasure Hunt*, M. J. Farrell and John Perry, John Gielgud, St. Martin's

19 June; *The Beggar's Opera*; John Gay, realised by Benjamin Britten; Tyrone Guthrie and Basil Coleman; Company of Four/Lyric Aldeburgh (designed with Christine Pirie)

9 August, *Captain Carvallo*, Denis Cannan, Laurence Olivier, St. James'

24 August, *Rosmersholm*, Henrik Ibsen, Michael MacOwen, St. Martin's

1951

3 March, *The Passing Day*, George Shiels, Tyrone Guthrie, Northern Ireland Festival Company/Lyric

24 March, *Richard II*, William Shakespeare, Anthony Quayle, Shakespeare (designed with Alix Stone)

3 April, *Henry IV, Part I*, William Shakespeare, Anthony Quayle and John Kidd, Shakespeare (designed with Alix Stone). Toured Australia and New Zealand, 1952-53.

8 May, *Henry IV, Part II*, William Shakespeare, Michael Redgrave, Shakespeare (designed with Alix Stone)

3 July, *The Passing Day*, George Shiels, Tyrone Guthrie, Northern Ireland Festival Company/Ambassadors

31 July, *Henry V*, William Shakespeare, Anthony Quayle, Shakespeare (designed with Alix Stone)

16 October, *Figure of Fun*, Andre Roussin, Peter Ashmore, Aldwych (costumes by Balmain)

26 December, *A Midsummer Night's Dream*, William Shakespeare, Tyrone Guthrie, Old Vic

1952–53

Planning Stratford Festival stage, Ontario

1952

6 March, *The Deep Blue Sea*, Terence Rattigan, Frith Banbury, Duchess

28 May, *Timon of Athens*, William Shakespeare, Tyrone Guthrie, Old Vic

1953

24 February, *Julius Caesar*, William Shakespeare, Hugh Hunt, Old Vic (costumes by Alan Tagg)

6 May, *Henry VIII*, William Shakespeare, Tyrone Guthrie, Old Vic

13 July, *Richard III*, William Shakespeare, Tyrone Guthrie, Stratford Festival

14 July, *All's Well That Ends Well*, William Shakespeare, Tyrone Guthrie, Stratford Festival

1954

16 March, *Othello*, William Shakespeare, Anthony Quayle, Shakespeare. Toured Australia and New Zealand, 1952-53.

28 June, *Measure for Measure*, William Shakespeare, Cecil Clarke, Stratford Festival

29 June, *The Taming of the Shrew*, William Shakespeare, Tyrone Guthrie, Stratford Festival

15 July, *Oedipus Rex*, Sophocles, Tyrone Guthrie, Stratford Festival. Revived 1955 at Stratford, toured to Assembly Hall and filmed, 1956.

28 August, *The Matchmaker*, Thornton Wilder, Tyrone Guthrie, Royal Lyceum

4 November, *The Matchmaker*, Thornton Wilder, Tyrone Guthrie, Royal Haymarket

1955

(?), *The Cherry Orchard*, Anton Chekhov, Giorgio Strehler, Piccolo

27 June, *Julius Caesar*, William Shakespeare, Michael Langham, Stratford Festival

29 June, *The Merchant of Venice*, William Shakespeare, Tyrone Guthrie, Stratford Festival

22 August, *A Life in the Sun*, Thornton Wilder, Tyrone Guthrie, Assembly Hall

27 October; *The Matchmaker*; Thornton Wilder; Tyrone Guthrie; Locust, Royale

1956–57

Modifications to Stratford Festival stage, permanent building

1956

18 June; *Henry V*; William Shakespeare; Michael Langham; Stratford Festival, Assembly Hall

19 June, *The Merry Wives of Windsor*, William Shakespeare, Michael Langham, Stratford Festival

14 August, *Measure for Measure*, William Shakespeare, Anthony Quayle, Shakespeare

1957

22 January, *The Two Gentlemen of Verona*, William Shakespeare, Michael Langham, Old Vic

2 July, *Twelfth Night*, William Shakespeare, Tyrone Guthrie, Stratford Festival

1958

12 February; *The Broken Jug*; Heinrich von Kleist, adapted by Don Harron; Michael Langham; Stratford Festival tour

14 February, *The Two Gentlemen of Verona*, William Shakespeare, Michael Langham, Stratford Festival tour

23 June, *Henry IV, Part I*, William Shakespeare, Michael Langham and George McCowan, Stratford Festival (designed with Marie Day)

21 July, *The Winter's Tale*, William Shakespeare, Douglas Campbell, Stratford Festival

26 August, *Much Ado About Nothing*, William Shakespeare, Douglas Seale, Shakespeare (costumes by Motley)

24 November, *The Bright One*, J. M. Fulton, Rex Harrison, Royal Brighton

12 December, *The Bright One*, J. M. Fulton, Rex Harrison, Winter Garden

1959

(?), *The Merchant of Venice*, William Shakespeare, Tyrone Guthrie, Habimah

(?), *Biedermann and the Fireraisers*, Max Frisch, Schrager Friedman, Habimah

21 April, *All's Well That Ends Well*, William Shakespeare, Tyrone Guthrie, Shakespeare

1960

2 February, *The Wrong Side of the Park*, John Mortimer, Peter Hall, Cambridge

27 June, *King John*, William Shakespeare, Douglas Seale, Stratford Festival

29 June, *Romeo and Juliet*, William Shakespeare, Michael Langham, Stratford Festival

1961–62

Modifications to Stratford Festival stage, with Brian Jackson

1961

12 January, *Ondine*, Jean Giraudoux, Peter Hall, Royal Shakespeare Company/Aldwych

19 June, *Coriolanus*, William Shakespeare, Michael Langham, Stratford Festival

21 June, *Love's Labour's Lost*, William Shakespeare, Michael Langham, Stratford Festival. Revived with Mark Negin (design) for tour to Chichester Festival Theatre 6 April 1964.

1962–63

Design of Guthrie Theater stage, Minneapolis

1962

19 June, *The Taming of the Shrew*, William Shakespeare, Michael Langham, Stratford Festival

30 July, *Cyrano de Bergerac*, Edmond Rostand, Michael Langham, Stratford Festival (designed with Desmond Heeley). Revived 1963.

28 November, *The Alchemist*, Ben Jonson, Tyrone Guthrie, Old Vic

1963–64

Renovation Avon Theatre, Stratford, Ontario

1963

(?), *The Three Sisters*, Anton Chekhov, Tyrone Guthrie, Guthrie

7 May, *Hamlet*, William Shakespeare, Tyrone Guthrie, Guthrie

8 May (?), *The Miser*, Molière, Douglas Campbell, Guthrie. Revived 1965 with Director Edward Payson Call.

1964

(?), *Saint Joan*, G. B. Shaw, Douglas Campbell, Guthrie

(?), *Volpone*, Ben Jonson, Tyrone Guthrie, Guthrie

1965

(?), *The Way of the World*, William Congreve, Douglas Campbell, Guthrie

(?), *The Cherry Orchard*, Anton Chekhov, Tyrone Guthrie, Guthrie

1966

(?), *As You Like It*, William Shakespeare, Edward Payson Call, Guthrie

(?), *The Skin of Our Teeth*, Thornton Wilder, Douglas Campbell, Guthrie (designed with Carolyn Parker)

1967

20 January; *Peter Grimes*; Benjamin Britten, text by Montagu Slater; Tyrone Guthrie; Metropolitan

21 July; *The House of Atreus*; Aeschylus, adapted by John Lewin; Tyrone Guthrie; Guthrie. Revived 1968, toured to Mark Taper Forum, Los Angeles and Billy Rose Theatre, New York (tour staging designed with John Jensen).

31 July, *Antony and Cleopatra*, William Shakespeare, Michael Langham, Stratford Festival

17 October, *Antony and Cleopatra*, William Shakespeare, Michael Langham, Expo '67

1968

16 January, *Volpone*, Ben Jonson, Tyrone Guthrie, National Theatre Company/Old Vic

1969

(?); *Macook's Corner*; George Shiels; Tyrone Guthrie; Ulster Theatre Company/Opera House, Abbey

1969

(?), *Swift*, Eugene McCabe, Tyrone Guthrie, Abbey

(?), *Uncle Vanya*, Anton Chekhov, Tyrone Guthrie, Guthrie

18 June, *The Caucasian Chalk Circle*, Bertolt Brecht, Colin George, Sheffield

1970–71

Consultant designer for Crucible Theatre, Sheffield

1970

21 July, *Cymbeline*, William Shakespeare, Jean Gascon, Stratford Festival

19 October, *Cymbeline*, William Shakespeare, Jean Gascon, National

1971

5 May, *The Barber of Seville*, Giacchino Rossini, Tyrone Guthrie, Phoenix Opera/Royal Brighton

1 December, *The Shoemaker's Holiday*, Thomas Decker, Douglas Campbell, Crucible

1972

29 February, *A Man For All Seasons*, Robert Bolt, Douglas Campbell, Crucible

4 October; *The Persians*; Aeschylus, adapted by John Lewin; Colin George; Crucible

1973

22 February; *The Misanthrope*; Molière, translated and adapted by Tony Harrison; John Dexter; National Theatre Company/Old Vic

5 April, *The Stirrings in Sheffield on Saturday Night*, Alan Cullen, Colin George, Crucible. Revived 27 August 1973.

(?), *The Government Inspector*, Nikolai Gogol, Michael Langham, Guthrie (set designed by John Jensen)

1974

15 February, *The Imaginary Invalid*, Molière, Jean Gascon, Stratford Festival tour to Australia

1975

10 March; *The Misanthrope*; Molière, translated and adapted by Tony Harrison; John Dexter; St. James

9 July; *The Misanthrope*; Molière, translated and adapted by Tony Harrison; John Dexter; Old Vic

9 September; *Phaedra Britannica*; Jean Racine, translated and adapted by Tony Harrison; John Dexter; National Theatre Company/Old Vic

1976

24 April; *The Voyage of Edgar Allan Poe*; Dominick Argento, libretto by Charles Nolte; H. Wesley Balk; Minnesota Opera Company/O'Shaughnessy. Revived at Morris A. Mechanic Theatre, Maryland, 1977.

31 October, *Rigoletto*, Giuseppe Verdi, John Dexter, Metropolitan

1977

6 June, *All's Well That Ends Well*, William Shakespeare, David Jones, Stratford Festival

1978

2 February, *Oedipus Rex* and *Oedipus at Colonnus*, Sophocles, Colin George, South Australia Theatre Company/Festival

27 September, *The Double Dealer*, William Congreve, Peter Wood, National Theatre Company/Olivier

1980

10 April, *Red Roses For Me*, Sean O'Casey, Hugh Hunt, Abbey

1981

(?), *Kidnapped in London*, Timothy Mason, Charles Nolte, Children's

17 March, *La Traviata*, Giuseppe Verdi, Colin Graham, Metropolitan

1982

6 August, *Mary Stuart*, Friedrich Schiller, John Hirsch, Stratford Festival (set design by Ming Cho Lee)

1983

(?), *King Lear*, William Shakespeare, Michael Elliott, Granada Television

5 August, *Tartuffe*, Molière, John Hirsch, Stratford Festival. Revived 13 July 1984.

1984

(?), *The Clandestine Marriage*, David Garrick and George Colman, Anthony Quayle, Compass Theatre Company/tour

7 June, *The Clandestine Marriage*, David Garrick and George Colman, Anthony Quayle, Albery

1985

9 August, *The Government Inspector*, Nikolai Gogol, Ronald Eyre, Stratford Festival (costumes designed with Polly Scranton Bohdanetzky)

Theater Abbreviations and Locations

Abbey   Abbey Theatre, Dublin
Adelphi   Adelphi Theatre, London
Albery   Albery Theatre, London
Aldeburgh   Aldeburgh Festival, Suffolk
Aldwych   Aldwych Theatre, London
Ambassadors   Ambassadors' Theatre, London
Apollo   Apollo Theatre, London
Arts in Cambridge   Arts in Cambridge, Cambridge, England
Assembly Hall   Assembly Hall, Edinburgh
Cambridge   Cambridge Theatre, London
Children's   Children's Theatre Company, Minneapolis
Comedy   Comedy Theatre, London
Crucible   Crucible Theatre, Sheffield
Davis   Davis Theatre, Croyden, England
Duchess   Duchess Theatre, London
Duke of York   Duke of York's Theatre, London
Embassy   Embassy Theatre, London
Expo '67   Expo '67, Montreal
Festival   Festival Playhouse, Adelaide
Granada Television   Granada Television, England
Guthrie   Guthrie Theater, Minneapolis
Habimah   Habimah, Tel Aviv
Liverpool   Liverpool Playhouse, Liverpool
Locust   Locust Street Theatre, Philadelphia
Lyric   Lyric Theatre, Hammersmith, England
Metropolitan   Metropolitan Opera, New York

National   National Arts Centre, Ottawa
New   New Theatre, London
O'Shaughnessy   O'Shaughnessy Auditorium, St. Paul
Old Vic   Old Vic Theatre, London
Olivier   Olivier Theatre, London
Opera House   Opera House, Belfast
Oxford   The Oxford Playhouse, Cambridge, England
People's Palace   People's Palace, Watford, England
Piccolo   Piccolo Teatro, Milan
Q   Q Theatre, London
Royal Lyceum   Royal Lyceum, Edinburgh
Royal Opera House   Royal Opera House, Covent Garden, London
Royale   Royale Theatre, New York
Sadler's Wells   Sadler's Wells Opera, London
Shakespeare   Shakespeare Memorial Theatre, Stratford-upon-Avon
Sheffield   Sheffield Playhouse
St. James   St. James Theatre, New York
St. James'   St. James' Theatre, London
St. Martin's   St. Martin's Theatre, London
Stratford Festival   Stratford Festival, Ontario
Royal Brighton   Theatre Royal, Brighton
Royal Haymarket   Theatre Royal, Haymarket, England
Royal Newcastle   Theatre Royal, Newcastle
Westminster   Westminster Theatre, London
Winter Garden   Winter Garden Theatre, London
Wyndham's   Wyndham's Theatre, London

PRODUCTION PHOTOGRAPHS

Don Getsug, "Lee Richardson as Apollo and Len Cariou as Orestes in *The House of Atreus*, Guthrie Theater, Minneapolis," 1967. Courtesy of Don Getsug Studios, *frontispiece*.

Photographer unknown, "Tanya Moiseiwitsch at the Abbey Theatre, Dublin," 1938. Courtesy of the Stratford Festival, Canada, *v*.

Angus McBean, "Michael Bates as Bardolph and Anthony Quayle as Falstaff in act 4, scene 2 of *Henry IV, Part I*, Shakespeare Memorial Theatre, Stratford-upon-Avon," 1951. Courtesy of the Harvard Theatre Collection, *vii*.

Angus McBean, "Michael Gwynn as the Duke of York, Alexander Gauge as the Earl of Northumberland, and Hugh Griffith as John of Gaunt in act 3, scene 5 of *Richard II*, Shakespeare Memorial Theatre, Stratford-upon-Avon," 1951. Courtesy of the Harvard Theatre Collection, *11*.

Don Getsug, "Robert Pastene as Aegisthus and Douglas Campbell as Clytemnestra present Agamemnon's body to the Furies in *The House of Atreus*, Guthrie Theater, Minneapolis," 1967. Courtesy of Don Getsug Studios, *color gallery*.

Tanya Moiseiwitsch (?), "Scene from *The Lost Leader*, Abbey Theatre, Dublin," 1937. Tanya Moiseiwitsch Collection, *43*.

Tanya Moiseiwitsch (?), "Fred Johnson as Timmy the Smith and Cyril Cusack as Martin Doul in the scene, 'Outside the Forge,' from *The Well of the Saints*, Abbey Theatre, Dublin," 1938. Tanya Moiseiwitsch Collection, *44*.

Tanya Moiseiwitsch (?), "Scene from *Casadh an t'Súgaín*, Abbey Theatre, Dublin," 1938. Tanya Moiseiwitsch Collection, *46*.

John Vickers, "Michael Warre as Christian and Ralph Richardson as Cyrano in *Cyrano de Bergerac*, Old Vic Theatre Company at the New Theatre, London," 1946. Courtesy of the John Vickers Theatre Collection, London, *53*.

John Vickers, "Margaret Leighton as Roxane, Michael Warre as Christian, and Ralph Richardson as Cyrano in the balcony scene, *Cyrano de Bergerac*, Old Vic Theatre Company at the New Theatre, London," 1946. Courtesy of the John Vickers Theatre Collection, London, *55*.

Angus McBean, "Peter Pears as Peter Grimes and Joan Cross as Ellen Orford in *Peter Grimes*, Royal Opera House, Covent Garden, London," 1947. Courtesy of Harvard Theatre Collection, *62*.

Angus McBean, "The Borough Company in act 1, scene 1 of *Peter Grimes*, Royal Opera House, Covent Garden, London," 1947. Courtesy of Harvard Theatre Collection, *63*.

Angus McBean, "Hubert Norville as Bob Boles, and Muriel Burnett and Blanche Turner as the nieces in *Peter Grimes*, Royal Opera House, Covent Garden, London," 1947. Courtesy of Harvard Theatre Collection, *65*.

Angus McBean, "Heather Stannard as the Queen; Heather Penwarden, Rachel Roberts, and Marjorie Steel as Ladies-in-Waiting; and Godfrey Bond and Edward Atienza as Gardeners in act 3, scene 4 of *Richard II*, Shakespeare Memorial Theatre, Stratford-upon-Avon," 1951. Courtesy of Harvard Theatre Collection, *74*.

Angus McBean, "Rosalind Atkinson as Mistress Quickly, Edward Atienza as Fang, Peter Henchie as Snare, Anthony Quayle as Falstaff, and Michael Bates as Bardolph in act 2, scene 1 of *Henry IV, Part II*, Shakespeare Memorial Theatre, Stratford-upon-Avon," 1951. Courtesy of Harvard Theatre Collection, *76*.

Angus McBean, "The company with Richard Burton as Henry V and Anthony Quayle as Falstaff in act 5, scene 5 of *Henry IV, Part II*, Shakespeare Memorial Theatre, Stratford-upon-Avon," 1951. Courtesy of Harvard Theatre Collection, *77*.

Peter Smith, "Alec Guinness as King Richard in *Richard III*, Stratford Festival, Ontario," 1953. Courtesy of the Stratford Festival, Canada, *88*.

Peter Smith, "Irene Worth as Queen Margaret in *Richard III*, Stratford Festival, Ontario," 1953. Courtesy of the Stratford Festival, Canada, *90*.

Herb Nott, "Jason Robards, Jr. as Polixenes, Powys Thomas as Camillo, Charmion King as Hermione, and Christopher Plummer as Leontes in *The Winter's Tale*, Stratford Festival, Ontario," 1958. Courtesy of the Stratford Festival, Canada, *100*.

Herb Nott, "Frances Hyland as Perdita in *The Winter's Tale*, Stratford Festival, Ontario," 1958. Courtesy of the Stratford Festival, Canada, *101*.

Herb Nott, "Eileen Herlie as Paulina, Charmion King as Hermione, and Sydney Sturgess and Deborah Turnbull as Ladies-in-Waiting in *The Winter's Tale*, Stratford Festival, Ontario," 1958. Courtesy of the Stratford Festival, Canada, *102*.

Don Getsug, "Douglas Campbell as Pallas Athena, Lee Richardson as Apollo, and Len Cariou as Orestes in *The House of Atreus*, Guthrie Theater, Minneapolis," 1967. Courtesy of Don Getsug Studios, *114*.

Don Getsug, "Lee Richardson as Agamemnon and Len Cariou as Orestes in *The House of Atreus*, Guthrie Theater, Minneapolis," 1967. Courtesy of Don Getsug Studios, *115*.

Don Getsug, "Lee Richardson as Agamemnon and Robin Gammell as Cassandra in *The House of Atreus*, Guthrie Theater, Minneapolis," 1967. Courtesy of Don Getsug Studios, *117*.

Anthony Crickmay, "Diana Rigg as the Memsahib, Alaknandra Samarth as Ayah, and Daniel Thorndike as Aide-de-Camp in *Phaedra Britannica*, National Theatre at the Old Vic, London," 1975. Collections of the Theatre Museum. By courtesy of the Board of Trustees of the Victoria and Albert Museum, London, *125*.

Anthony Crickmay, "Alaknandra Samarth as Ayah and Diana Rigg as the Memsahib in *Phaedra Britannica*, National Theatre at the Old Vic, London," 1975. Collections of the Theatre Museum. By courtesy of the Board of Trustees of the Victoria and Albert Museum, London, *126*.